DATE DUE

Demco, Inc. 38-293

Plan to Succeed

A Guide to Strategic Planning

Steven C. Stryker

GOVERNMENT INSTITUTES
AN IMPRINT OF
THE SCARECROW PRESS, INC.
Lanham • Toronto • Plymouth, UK
2012

 **Government Institutes**

Published by Government Institutes
An imprint of The Scarecrow Press, Inc.
A wholly owned subsidiary of The Rowman & Littlefield Publishing Group, Inc.
4501 Forbes Boulevard, Suite 200, Lanham, Maryland 20706
http://www.govinstpress.com

Estover Road, Plymouth PL6 7PY, United Kingdom

British Library Cataloguing in Publication Information Available

Library of Congress Cataloging-in-Publication Data
Stryker, Steven C.
  Plan to succeed : a guide to strategic planning / Steven C. Stryker.
    p. cm.
  Rev. ed. of: Plan to succeed : a guide to strategic planning. c1986
  Includes index.
  ISBN 978-1-60590-727-7 (cloth : alk. paper) — ISBN 978-1-60590-728-4 (elec)
  1. Strategic planning. I. Title.
HD30.28.S78 2012
658.4'012—dc23   2011038529

♾™ The paper used in this publication meets the minimum requirements of American National Standard for Information Sciences—Permanence of Paper for Printed Library Materials, ANSI/NISO Z39.48-1992.

Printed in the United States of America

For Don Philpott—who showed me that true planning is saying "why not" and then bringing to light valuable information—again!

Contents

Preface

"The more things change, the more they stay the same," said the cynical philosopher. With over a hundred years of modern business experience, thousands of books, articles and reports and millions of business consulting hours, the same mistakes are being made and pitfalls are occurring in not effectively responding to change and solving problems. Why? Is there still a "dearth" of simple and useful tools? Is human nature such that when people get into business they lose their ability to handle situations successfully? Or is the profit motive satisfied without the need to handle threats or opportunities? The answer to the first question is what this volume is all about. People are still getting into business, experiencing growth and success, facing crises or problems, surviving for years and even leaving their business with a hefty profit without integrating planning to the essence of firm activities.

This volume is written to provide a new direction and capability for planning.

The kind of planning discussed herein is strategic planning—that is, planning to handle problems and opportunities which the firm will face day in and day out as it strives to achieve its goals and objectives—in both the short and long term!

Many small business owners and operators are reluctant to practice this kind of planning. Their focus instead is to make the business "work."

Yet is getting a business to "work" enough to keep it viable in the increasingly turbulent business climate today? Where there is risk there must be some thoughts of response to it. Where there is increased risk, thoughts need to turn to action to positively deal with it today, tomorrow and beyond.

Much planning deals with how to think ahead and respond better now. This volume takes this idea a step further as a self-training guide to both learning and immediately applying the insights gained for the life cycle of your business situation.

Such applications include being able to:

- Identify opportunities and/or threats facing your firm and having an ability to respond to them.
- Discover strengths and/or weaknesses coming from inside your firm and understanding what to do with them.
- Demonstrate the contingencies of business operations so as to know how to handle them beforehand.
- Understand what needs to be done to achieve your company's purpose, goals, objectives and mission.
- Assess whether you can be successful with your firm now or in the future.
- Transmit strategic planning skills to all members as their contributions become central to improving and expanding operations.
- Have strategic planning become integral to your organization's growth and development.

For the bottom line is not maximum profits; instead, it is to survive in the most completely satisfying ways all members decide.

Further, this "how-to" guide to coping with everyday changes does not stop once the business begins. Instead, strategic planning is demonstrated at each stage of the firm's evolution from conception to maturity—to show what are the concerns which you may conceivably face in operating during that time period. So, whether you are not in business yet, have been in business for two years, or five years, or left the business environment and are now returning, you can read ahead to see beforehand what are those future issues for which preparations can be made now to deal with. All strategic issues are listed in the Contents. (In fact, some of the issues mentioned during one stage may occur for your business at an earlier or later stage. For this reason, it is a good idea to read over the entire book to familiarize yourself with the gamut of issues and their alternative ways of being resolved.) Thus, the information in each chapter can be of use to you whatever business development stage your company faces now. Don't needlessly skip an early chapter if your business is in a later stage. This book can be of large benefit to:

- new business founders or operators.
- existing owners or managers.
- current organizational members considering a career move.

- consultants wishing to expand their advisory services to small businesses.
- trainers or facilitators wishing to use this volume as a lucid medium for learning.

Special thanks go to Bruce Martin, Research Facilities Division, Library of Congress, for the privilege of using the collections, and Gwen Davis, Friday's Girl Service, Silver Spring, Maryland, for composing the manuscript with incredible speed and accuracy. Also, a particular note of recognition to Elizabeth A. Bunn, whose dancing school business and strategic plan formed the basis of the sample company discussed in chapters 5-10. In addition, Teri, Rick, Debbie and their spouses deserve thanks for encouraging and strengthening my motivation.

The skills and principles discussed herein are not limited to only one kind of business, one size of business, one structure of business, or one attitude of business. Anyone who seeks better ways of making his or her business thrive should be able to benefit from the time spent digesting and using the material herein. Yet do not take my word alone. For, like any effective learning device, this book will not "have the answers," but will hopefully provide the catalysts through which you can find them for yourself as your business progresses. As Tehyi Hsieh said long ago in a book titled *Chinese Epigrams*, "The key to success isn't much good until one discovers the right lock to insert it in."

Have fun and much success with the exploration!

Steven C. Stryker
Rockville, Maryland

Chapter 1

Discovering Strategic Planning

SNAPSHOT

Planning began when a person said, "If I had known more, I should/could have handled this situation better than I did." From this hindsight motif, we realized that if we don't learn from experiences we are bound to repeat the same mistakes. And since business success is based on doing the right things right, some forethought ought to be given to how these "things" can be accomplished. Yet, speak to the alter-egos of many business owners today and you will likely find several or more "I Cannots," as shown in Exhibit 1-1 following. These statements become justification for ignoring, downplaying or negating the strategic planning activity. If these observations were all truthful, sensible and success stimulants, there would be nothing to write about in this book. Business would go on as usual. Instead, this chapter will present past experience as the perspective to seriously reconsider the thoughts in Exhibit 1-1.

Subsequent chapters will also handle those objections for which answers have been illusive.

DOES DOING STRATEGIC PLANNING MAKE SENSE?

Four instances of how business grows are shown in the following sections to illustrate strategic planning. Each instance is taken from an actual company, with the names and events changed for quick description. The dynamics of planning are actual in each case.

Exhibit 1-1 Litany of I Cannot

- I do not have time. I am too busy struggling with crises.
- I do not see the benefits to my firm or me.
- I do not know how.
- I have seen enough business successes to know I do not need it.
- I will not spend the money.
- I do not have the staff required to do it.
- I have no secrets to hide.
- I do not need to lobby Washington.
- I do not want to become the largest company in the market.
- I can do fine without discovering every tax loophole I uncover.
- I do not need to justify my continued leadership to outsiders.
- I understand what I need to know to survive.
- I was not taught the "business ropes"; instead, I learned the hard, best way—from the street.
- I know that if I do real well today, that I can carryover success for tomorrow.
- I do not need to support a large bureaucracy.
- I do not depend on planning for answers, but for people.
- I leave it to the Fortune 500 to do.
- I compete against only one other party—myself.
- I am beholden to no one, and so why have a plan?
- I have not found a technique applicable to each step of my firm's progress.
- I have no commitment to it.

Company One: The Yellow Veranda

Set back 100 yards from a four-chambered pond, this rustic country inn has been operating well for three years. Purchased from a widow (whose family had lived there for three generations) by Eloise Newhouse, the restaurant began to turn a profit in the fourth quarter of its first operating year. How was she able to accomplish this feat in an industry where two years is not an uncommon time before a profit is turned? As she said, her success is based on strong and complete strategic planning. The genesis of her success are the forethoughts and actions she did long before opening the doors of The Yellow Veranda. First, she created a vision of her business: a place where harried urbanites could come and relax with the right combination of good food, pleasant surroundings, old-world charm, personal service and competitive prices. Next, she went out and got experience. Leaving her stockbroker position, she first became a hostess and assistant food buyer at a friend's summer dinner theater. When it closed down for the winter, she found a position as an assistant manager and chef at a boutique restaurant in the revived downtown area. She worked for half the normal salary in order to gain much more than money—experience and incentive to open her own place.

In her spare time, during this eighteen-month apprenticeship, she slowly put together her first strategic plan for her business. She carefully culled information about country inn restaurants from books, restaurateurs, consultants, patrons, associations, and the Small Business Administration. What she found was data about everything from furnishings to budgeting to marketing to menu design to lease financing to location and size. In addition, after touring several sites, Eloise selected the area and location she'd like. She later had discussions with the present owner of what was to become The Yellow Veranda to find out whether she would lease or buy. Taking all the numbers, forms, descriptions and future actions, Eloise produced a strategic plan which explained when and how she would open the business as well as how much money she needed and from which sources.

The proof of the pudding of the first strategic plan is obtaining the resources needed to get started. Money requirements were estimated at about $250,000 for the first year. Eloise applied to the First Federal Bank in her area and to the SBA for loans totaling 75% of the amount.

She brought a three-year financial projection, equipment and inventory requirements, locational expenses and refurbishing costs, salary and utility expenses, projected demand, pricing, marketing tactics, clientele served, hiring and retaining employees, quality controls, and her resume—together, the strategic plan. The information presented was thorough, substantiated and complete. In addition, she put up her own funds to acquire a lease, to obtain a business license, and retain a lawyer and an accountant. Finally, her strategic plan discussed how she would modify the planning efforts to direct the next steps of operation and eventual growth. She obtained the financing she required, did turn a profit before the first year ended and is today, at 2.5 years into restaurateuring, thinking of opening another country inn.

Company Two: Cleanside, Inc.

Eight years ago, two entrepreneurs had a simple but brilliant idea: contract out the dirty work. Focused on the nursing home sector, this firm provides cost-effective housekeeping, maintenance and repair services for all areas of a facility. The problem, as founder James Foreman saw it, was that janitors and other maintenance people got "no respect among staff," were poorly trained since "anyone can keep a place clean," and lacked any career incentives in most nursing home situations. His solution was to offer well-trained managers who knew how to motivate their staffs and interface well with facility personnel. All Cleanside employees go through training and are shown the means to career advancement through increasingly responsible management assignments. The performance evaluations are rigorous, but tailored to the growth of each member of the firm. This system has paid off in spades: with over seventy contracts last year, the firm earned a 16% profit. In the last four years, net earnings have doubled each year, and only seven clients have not renewed their contracts in the firm's history.

There is a latent demand for such services, which has been increasing rapidly. Capital concerns are insignificant since cash flow starts with the first client payment and a recent public offering netted the company $3.25 million. The only constraint to unabashed growth is management training, availability and performance. When the business volume taxed management's capacity to manage (at any level), James Foreman put a moratorium on obtaining more contracts. This action caused the company to lose new contracts in two instances, but allowed the existing contracts to be handled properly.

Shortcuts could be taken. More accounts can be handled by fewer managers. Management training can be reduced and succession time cut. More potential managers can be obtained through acquisition of similar companies. Each manager can be responsible for more people under his or her control. Yet, all these alternatives fly in the face of the strategic plan. James Foreman wants to stick to the strategic plan. He has seen how it helped direct the success of the company. He knows that deviation from "the plan" is easy; yet, while it drives growth, it also constrains it. In fact, one of the greatest threats to the firm's long-term survival Foreman dubs "impatience"—the urge to shortcut the plan. Thus, when future growth occurs at Cleanside, Inc., it will be solidly based and carried out.

Company Three: Compu-Net, Ltd., Partners Evelen Krasnow and Lawrence Phelps

Phelps knew they had a better idea for a telecommunications networking system. Having worked for key Silicon Valley companies, Krasnow and Phelps spent two years developing a strategic plan that predicted that the industry market will decline in the next five years. Unlike Cleanside, Inc., which sold a solution to a problem, Compu-Net, Ltd., found a solution waiting for a problem. Their solution was a means of inter-computer information transfer. The strategic marketing route chosen was to have firm growth determined by market demand, so that sales will lead expenses.

The first months of revenue were lower than expected from the strategic plan, as Krasnow and Phelps imposed a retrenchment program which included a hiring freeze, marketing and distribution objectives, and minimal employee business expenses. Shortly thereafter, a pay cut was taken by everyone. However, a new microcomputer line came out two months later. The manufacturer contacted Compu-Net, Ltd., and after seeing a demonstration of the network software, decided to feature it as part of the offered software packages. With this turnaround came a refocus on the strategic plan—to stick closely to the original corporate purpose and do what it takes to keep turnover low. The thrust, according to Krasnow, is long-term profitable growth instead of short-term market share.

Company Four: Simon, Montez and Associates

Jill Simon and Carlos Montez seemed like an unlikely match for architectural partners. Simon, a ten-year award-winning architect of commercial properties and Montez, a five-year technical draftsman with industrial plants to his credit, saw plenty of inefficiencies, office politics, and overcharging that degraded the quality of new structures. They developed a system of marketing, designing, and quality control which became the centerpiece of their strategic plan. Simon did the marketing; Montez provided the technical support to book the engagement. Their approach was to provide professional results as a service business, yet to do so in a self-motivated environment with incentives and tolerance for new ideas.

The firm's philosophy was do all facets well, integrate them better and provide innovation at competitive prices.

Putting the strategic plan to work meant targeting their market: the partners chose governmental work. They won a design competition with the city for a bus vehicle maintenance center. This was completed by the partners and new associates who worked part time on the project and freelanced the rest of the time. The center won five awards and led to the surge in marketing energy exerted by Simon. The next contract was from a federal agency for a series of vehicle maintenance centers. The specifications called for designs presented in computer graphic form. The firm used computer-aided design and drafting, finished the assignment on time, within budget and with a software marketing tool. This "tool" spiraled client interest for state-of-the-art architecture. In one month, more fees poured in than in the previous year. The work kept coming, a new subsidiary was set up to sell computerized architecture, engineering and drafting services, and the firm kept moving to larger quarters to have places for the steady inflow of new hires.

During this meteoric growth phase, the strategic planning focused on how to keep productivity high. Simon and Montez reorganized the firm into project teams, disregarding the departmental approach. In this way clients could access a project in any of its stages and provide more interactive teamwork among the architects, engineers, designers and accountants. The actions worked: productivity rose to $50,000 per employee, 25% higher than the industry average, and profits were 3.5 times greater than industry average. Yet, these accomplishments were done in the first three years of the firm's existence.

Then, a recession finally arrived, and like a hurricane, hit hard and fast. The firm lost three projects in a row and the backlog dropped from twelve to two months. New projects came fewer and farther between with smaller fees per engagement. The firm retrenched and slowly began preparing for long-term survival.

This last example was chosen since it illustrates one of the classical flaws of strategic planning: partial application. Simon, Montez and Associates believed in planning, but only as a force to go from A to B once A, B and the speed of getting there are determined. The experience of the other firms presented shows differently: growth is only one measure of business success among many. When entrepreneurs become fixated on growth so that it becomes both a means and an end, then firm survival is put into jeopardy. In fact, it is just strategic planning which can regulate how fast your firm should grow for long-term survival.

*   *   *

This volume's purpose is to clearly and completely demonstrate how integrated strategic planning can assist in creating the particular, effective balance of present actions and future options a firm requires to achieve broad and deep long-term business success.

To achieve this purpose the book is divided into nine additional chapters. Chapter 2 presents the strategic planning technique while chapter 3 defines the new company and the entrepreneurial qualities to make it go. Chapter 4 displays the major concept in this book: the elements comprising the stages of a firm's growth and development. This life cycle precept is combined with the strategic planning technique in each of chapters 5–10 to unlock the major issues a firm needs to recognize and address during each phase of its evolution. In each chapter there are several Sample Tasks that enable you to immediately drive home the concept, process or technique that is just discussed as well as build upon previous topics. Also, to demonstrate the full business viability, a "live" firm's attempts with strategic planning are described respectively in the latter chapters.

Chapter 2

Preparing for Strategic Planning

SNAPSHOT

"Strategic planning is a foreign discipline to many smaller or medium-sized companies. It is . . . rarely learned or mastered by self-taught entrepreneurs."[1] These statements signify a lack of interest and skill in applying strategic planning to small businesses. Could it be that some owners and operators of small companies know something the rest of us don't? After all, new firms sprout, flourish, and grow all the time. And even though the single largest cause of business failure is poor management and the number of failures is on the rise, many companies make it without strategic planning.

Why should the small business owner crowd his already hectic schedule with yet another task? A partial answer to this question was given in the last chapter—the increasing rate of new developments and changes affecting small businesses demand a suitable and effective means to respond. More importantly, you can't be a success without strategic planning. Sure, if you give a monkey a typewriter and enough paper and time, the animal could type a section of the Bible. Likewise, if an entrepreneur puts dollars, technology, people, and skills on the line and happens to steer just the right course through the minefield of unknowns awaiting her demise, then all will work out well. However, most smart, savvy business persons do not want to take such a large risk.

Another objection to strategic planning is that "small businesses have no track record in using strategic planning." Absolutely not. There are reports, articles, and interviews about traditional and innovative small companies that used strategic planning from inception to large-scale success.

The third objection, "It will be too costly to use this technique. Our resources are severely limited, and we are not in a position to use any sophisticated techniques." Yes, strategic planning is likely to cost more, but it is
easily understood, quickly learned, and readily applied to existing operations.

In this chapter, we define the concept, process, results, and assumptions of
strategic planning. All of these elements make up the road map for picturing
and comprehending the essence of this book. As with most written works, this
one has a bias. It is that if the Fortune 500 companies need strategic planning
somewhat, and large companies need it a great deal, then small businesses
must use it to sustain their very survival.

DEFINITION AND TERMINOLOGY

If you are going to successfully practice strategic planning, you first need to
understand the terms. Much has been written on this subject, but much of it
is vague because the words are not well-defined.

In fact, one prolific writer in this area even used the words he was trying
to define in his definition! Thus, we need to separate the "wheat" from the
"chaff" concerning strategic planning.

First, why are semantics a hindrance?

The following terms are often used to describe strategic planning: *strategy,
policy, business policy, long-range planning, corporate planning, strategy
management*, and *strategic management*. In many cases, these terms are used
interchangeably with no apparent regard for their different meanings.

Each term has a distinct meaning and cannot be loosely substituted.

Let's consider *strategy*. This is a master plan that specifies critical courses
of action and the means to accomplish three ends:

- to achieve objectives established by the organization;
- to exploit opportunities and strengths; and
- to counteract present and future threats and weaknesses.

Strategy management is the process and controls used to create and execute strategy. *Strategic* refers to the use of strategy and strategy management
in a particular business environment. So, *strategic planning* is the anticipa-
tion and resolution of a particular firm's problems using the tools developed
by strategy and strategy management. (In many writings, *strategy* refers to
the methods used to cure business ills or strengthen business health. *Strategy
management* is the way management performs these methods. Using these
terms in this way severely limits their effectiveness.)

Second, why is strategic planning so misunderstood?

Strategic planning is thought to mean the creation of "pictures" of how the organization should appear five, ten, twenty, or twenty-five years hence. That is, strategic planning becomes identical with long-range planning. Long-range planning describes what the future could be without much, if any, sense of how to bring about that future. Strategic planning deals in the here and now in trying to create and fulfill the design for tomorrow.

Third, what is strategic planning all about?

Many authors use strategic planning and business policy interchangeably. However, business policies are guidelines for decision making by management. Such guidelines are developed after a strategic planning activity is underway, and they are used to support the implementation of the strategic plan. To sum up, strategic planning is a unique and precise term describing a dynamic activity for accomplishing an organization's stated purpose.

Sample Task 1

Based on the discussion thus far, sit down with pencil and paper and make a list of reasons why strategic planning might be useful and why it might not. Have at least three reasons for each side. Evaluate your responses. Are you likely to continue reading? Why?

Process and Results

A definition is only as good as its attempted application. In this section, we will show you how to develop a strategic plan. Although the steps described are general, their specific use is particular to your company. Exhibit 2-1 presents the blueprint for strategic planning. Each phase is described in more detail in subsequent chapters, but, for now, is as follows:

A. Define the business. This definition will include the following:

1. Statement of Purpose. What is the specific nature of your business, and what is its end result?
2. Goals. What does the firm want to achieve over its lifetime of operation?
3. Objectives. What does the firm want to achieve in the short term?
4. Mission. What is the firm's sense of social responsibility?

Together these four terms give substance, direction, and meaning to the firm. In stronger language, without knowing who you are or where you're going, strategic planning will have little use.

Chapter 2

Exhibit 2-1

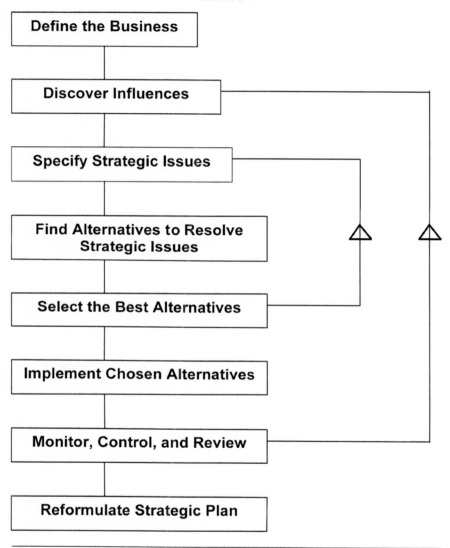

B. Discover influences. Next, determine what outside influences affect the company or will affect its operation. This information is collected through current information analysis and the study of the firm's internal operations, structure, and morale.

Together, the collected information forms an "influence database."

C. Specify strategic issues. At this point, the influence database is used to produce concrete statements of the particular concerns facing the company. These factual sentences are then ranked in importance according to the definition of the firm.

D. Find alternatives to resolve strategic issues.

Come up with a wide array of plausible means to resolve the strategic issues.

E. Select the best alternatives. First establish the decision criteria used to select alternatives. The criteria will be partially quantitative and partially qualitative.

Next, use the criteria to eliminate any undesirable alternatives, and then choose among the remaining alternatives. Examine the set of chosen alternatives and verify that the firm's future direction is reflected. That is, does the alternative help the firm to grow, stabilize, or survive? And is this direction consistent with the state of your business?

F. Implement chosen alternatives. Here the alternatives are turned into actions to resolve the strategic issues. Specific tasks are defined, resources gathered and people assigned.

G. Monitor, control, and review. During the implementation stage, correct and reinforce any action. After a given time period, assess the results and make improvements. Review the progress made and give presentations about the efforts.

H. Reformulate strategic plan. At the end of the planning cycle, update the influence database. Next, discover new strategic issues. Combine these with unresolved ones from the old strategic plan to formulate and execute a subsequent version.

This process is straightforward and doable. Yet, many, if not most, small business owners and managers find lots of excuses not to use it. There is only one excuse that works: a lack of desire for sustained success and an inability to change.

The outcome of a strategic planning effort is a set of actions to resolve strategic issues. In addition, if there is trouble in choosing among alternatives, it may reflect the way the strategic issues were defined. Or, if the monitoring and control phase turns up some large problems, it may reflect the accuracy and reliability of the influence database. In either case, a return to that phase, proper checking, and modifications may be necessary (see Exhibit 2-1).

The strategic planning document (Exhibit 2-2) is the firm's attempt to provide a usable and flexible approach to strategic planning. Note that it is designed for more than one strategic plan, for example, at the corporate as well as the department level. The document also includes a section on contingency plans, shortened strategic plans developed to ask and answer "what if" questions that could prevent the firm from carrying out its objectives or strategic planning effort. (A further discussion of this topic appears in chapter 7.)

Sample Task 2

Pick a strategic issue of great importance to your firm at this time. Perform strategic planning. Assess the outcome—are you in a better position to handle the strategic issue? Why?

Exhibit 2-3 is a practical illustration of a strategic plan (according to Exhibit 2-2) for a small company. The mechanics will be covered in subsequent chapters. Nonetheless, the items presented demonstrate that a team of experts and a flock of wizards are not prerequisites to doing strategic planning well. This volume is concerned with whether the motivation exists to do strategic planning, not whether the intelligence does.

Exhibit 2-2 Strategic Planning Document

I. **Statement of Need for Strategic Planning**
II. **Guidelines for Carrying out Strategic Planning**
III. **Primary Company Information**
    A. Definition of the firm
    B. Influence database
IV. **Strategic Plans**
    A. Strategic issues
    B. Alternatives to resolve strategic issues
    C. Decision criteria and choice
    D. Implementation of alternatives
    E. Monitoring, control, and review
V. **Reformulation of Strategic Plans**
VI. **Contingency Plans**
VII. **Appendices**
    A. Reference data
    B. Bibliography
    C. Supporting evidence
       - environmental analyses
       - studies of issues
       - legal documents
       - estimates of _____

Exhibit 2-3 Example of a Strategic Plan

Company Name: Inventcon, Inc.

Company Purpose: Design and development of computer software to solve various inventory control problems.

Strategic Issues

1. Market demand diminishing for this type of software.
2. Many companies developing such software in house.
3. Many companies requiring such software are modifying data-processing functions.
4. Compatibility of software with existing computer hardware and software in each firm.
5. Competition requires multiple advertising media and flexible pricing structure.

Alternatives to Resolve Strategic Issues

1. Target market segments that have not been reached before.
2. Take more personal approach to marketing.
3. Ensure that software can be made to run on client's computer equipment.
4. Offer additional software services such as computer, system design, telecommunications requirement analysis, or hardware/software selection.
5. Expand inventory features offered in software.
6. Team up with manufacturer of computer hardware to sell Inventcon software.

Decision Criteria

1. Time to implement.
2. Cost to implement.
3. Compatibility with firm's purpose.
4. Previous applications of alternative.
5. Degree to which status quo can be returned to if alternative is not successful.

Choice

1. Alternatives 2, 3, and 5 are picked.

Implementation

1. Discover previous clients or potential clients who might need services.
2. Contact each client to discuss future needs.
3. Gain admission by taking a survey of inventory software requirements.
4. Upgrade software capabilities by having modules ready to run on client's hardware.
5. Increase number of inventory control problems that can be handled using software.

(continued)

Exhibit 2-3 (Continued)

Monitoring, Control, and Review

1. Assess marketing effort after three months. If performance is not what is expected (three new clients), then expand outreach activity. If performance is what is expected, ensure inventory software needs are met in comprehensive fashion.
2. Solve any compatibility problems with client's computer system.
3. Ensure rigorous testing of new software modules is done before being made available to clients.
4. Review all activities after 180 days. Assess whether technical and marketing performance is what is targeted. If so, continue market penetration and software upgrade. If not, carefully define areas of improvement, and carry out strategic planning process to reflect these changes.

Sample Task 3

Take a hard look at Exhibit 2-2. Can this design be used for both new and existing companies? Why? List five ways that you could use this design in your firm.

Assumptions

Since we are going to spend the rest of this book discussing how to formulate, implement, and modify strategic plans, it is useful at this point to discuss the factors that "drive" the strategic planning process.

Exhibit 2-4 presents the premises that help start, develop, and sustain the strategic planning process. As the exhibit demonstrates, strategic planning charts direction for the firm. It does not make decisions; rather, it gives members the pertinent information to make better decisions. If used properly, strategic planning won't become rigid or relegated to one area of the firm's activities; instead, it will continue to be a well spring of creative questions and answers to company concerns.

Further, the process and tools of strategic planning are not likely to become irrelevant; they will be used time and again to serve the changing needs of an evolving organization. Yet, in order to be effective, strategic planning requires the support of all the firm's members and the active participation of the president. In addition, the process is flexible enough to incorporate changes that occur during its implementation. The upshot of this effort is a stronger organization better able to meet its market demands and to provide a viable work environment for its members.

Exhibit 2-4 Premises Governing Strategic Planning

Premise	Implications
General Use	Where are we? Where do we want to go? How will we get there? Who will be responsible? How much will it cost? When will it happen?
Flexible Process	Dynamic Responsive to change Participatory Encourages innovation
Useful Results	Solves company difficulties Generates new opportunities Ensures longer-term survival
Total Involvement	CEO leads and designs climate for self-examination Members of firm encouraged to participate and give feedback
Wide Applicability	Problem-solving technique for any type of concern at any organizational level
Encompasses All Planning Activates	Charts direction for firm Uses short-term acts as prelude to longer-term successes
Stimulates Better Interaction	Involves entire company Deals with resistance to change or conflicts with innovation
Cyclical Activity	Done using same steps at regular intervals Will evolve as reflection of firm's development Application will also cause firm to evolve
Good for Any Age Firm	Done before firm's doors are opened Done during start up Done during growth Done after several years of operation Done for firms in crisis or showing signs of trouble

Sample Task 4

Examine Exhibit 2-4. What premises are you already using in your firm? Which ones do you want to use? Which premises would be difficult to use? Why? Is not using these premises likely to hinder the positive results of strategic planning? Why?

Case Study

How fast, how far, how smart?

   High Resolve, Inc., was in a jam. As one of the first entrants into the industrial lasers market, it appears that "factors beyond its control" have turned its silver lining gray. Founded by two optical engineers, Helen and Joe Wright-Waye, the company placed all of its initial efforts into developing a high-resolution device for a chemical client. If this firm was totally satisfied, the laser could then be produced and marketed to other firms in the chemical industry. As it turned out, this first client was very pleased with the laser and even suggested other companies to contact. High Resolve, Inc., started producing the laser and opening marketing offices in Dallas, Atlanta, Chicago, and Boston. Yet higher-than-anticipated start-up costs and over-optimistic market penetration targets squeezed the cash flow. Helen Wright-Waye summed up the concern by noting that "we had a production plant to support, and we needed $50,000 to 60,000 each month from each office just to break even. We were also newcomers and didn't have a track record." Further, the chemical industry was beginning to experience an economic downturn that meant cutbacks in capital expenditures just as High Resolve was marketing its new product. Also, a technical problem with the resolution component required a redesign which, in turn, added to the debt burden. "It appears that everything we do is thwarted," says Joe. "If we can only keep all the parts functioning, we'll be in great shape."

   The following week an article appeared in *Optical Monthly* about a laser similar to the one High Resolve is producing. However, this laser was being successfully marketed to oil companies as well as natural gas companies.

   This case study clearly reflects that High Resolve, Inc., did not articulate, analyze, and structure a sense of direction to accomplish their objectives. Wishing and muddling through are clearly two modes of operation that don't work.

SUMMARY AND EXTENSION

It is possible to conclude that strategic planning is the "wonder drug" for your organization. After all, it is the means by which any situation that blocks or stifles your organization's success is identified and quickly dealt with. It is also the way your organization can learn of opportunities and quickly respond to make a sizable profit. But, strategic planning doesn't come with unconditional guarantees. It provides a method and a plan to increase the probability of success in dealing with today's business situation because it teaches you how to identify and respond to such situations. The antiquated means of (1) reacting only when there's a crisis or (2) why worry about tomorrow if everything is okay today fail to fulfill the firm's definition. Strategic planning does not just solve problems, it incorporates ways of conduct for present and future activities. As illustrated in the Case Study, hoping, complaining, and putting on blinders prevents you from coping with unforeseen events, client changes, and competition.

The bottom line is clear: "The unwillingness to give such planning the time it requires reflects a willingness to sacrifice the future for the present, and a lack of understanding of the fact that most of the urgent matters requiring attention now are consequences of inadequate planning in the past. Only planning can provide escape from crisis management."[2]

The principal obstruction between us and the future is *us*.

NOTES

1. Larry E. Greiner and Robert O. Metzger, *Consulting to Management*. Englewood Cliffs, NJ: Prentice-Hall, Inc., 1983, p. 92.

2. Russell L. Ackoff, *Creating the Corporate Future—Plan or Be Planned For*. New York: John Wiley & Sons, Inc., 1981, p. 240.

Chapter 3

Defining the Firm

SNAPSHOT

The previous chapter introduced and explained the concept of strategic planning. Its primary use is to solve business problems for companies which are conceived or currently operating. However, before we can address the strategic planning needs of such firms, two tasks must be performed:

1. We need to conceptualize and decide on which kind of business to be in.
2. We must understand the length and breath of growth possibilities for the company.

The first task is self-evident. Since no firm can operate until it's defined, first things first. The second task is not as immediately seen. If strategic planning is truly to have both an everyday and long-term impact on the firm's success, a life cycle orientation is a basic requirement prior to beginning strategic planning. This chapter will address the means to define which business to do. Chapter 4 will focus on the second task. Herein, we'll describe a method for recognizing, understanding, and responding to the characteristics and talents of would-be business people to glean business choices which match such characteristics and talents. The bottom line is your ability to effectively assess whether you have got the makings of a successful person in business.

PORTRAYING A FUTURE BUSINESS PERSON

The first mark of any firm is an idea for a business. Most people come up with "the" idea through no set or common means. And the number of successful businesses attest that a random selection of the idea works fine. But, was the idea found purely through inspiration? Isn't there some method to the madness of discovering the business to pursue? The answers are that inspiration is a necessary, but not sufficient, ingredient in deciding which business to pursue. Most persons who have hit on a successful business idea have done so by being informed as well as inspired. Thus, as shown in Exhibit 3-1, there is a rational means to move from an inkling to an articulated sense of potential business.

The first step toward knowing the business for you to be in is to understand why you want to be in business at all. Exhibit 3-2 presents some of the more common motivations. Positive or negative situations can spawn these motivations. Yet, whether being your own business person means getting away from something or moving toward something, the common drives are for money, satisfaction and achievement. Ok, so the next step is to find the conduit to obtain these objectives? Yes, but not by merely jumping into a business. Why? Knowing what you would like to do is a long way from accomplishing it. To make your business happen requires more than just knowing your goals and objectives—it also requires insight and understanding into whether you have the entrepreneurial characteristics to decide on a business and the small-business talents to operate a business.

Exhibit 3-3 gives the first part of the answer: characteristics of entrepreneurs. Before opening a business, you need to recognize that there are attributes and abilities which describe a potential business person much the same way as attributes and abilities are used to describe an artist, teacher, sports person, diplomat, etc. At this point, you are wondering whether Exhibit 3-3 is a candy-coated bunch of bunk. What the qualities and skills concretely demonstrate is those concerns which need to be considered prior to discovering a business to get involved with. Why?

If these concerns are down played, short cutted or ignored, strategic issues will arise sooner and be potentially disruptive of business operations, will mean loss of customers or clients, impede business growth, or indefinitely constrain the full achievement of the motivations in Exhibit 3-2. On the other hand, this pool of characteristics gives you a strong sense of what it will take to become a person in business and later a successful business person.

Given that you see the creative sensitivities needed to effectively behave in business situations, Exhibit 3-4 shows the capabilities for operating a firm. Notice that in sections II through V of Exhibit 3-4, the primary acumen is

Exhibit 3-1

Exhibit 3-2 Motivating Influences for Going Into Business

- Ability to be a financial success in a way unlike any other.
- Desire to be own boss and master, direct and chart course of an organization and take credit for making substantive contributions to society.
- Opportunity and challenge to make something work, to work with people and to sustain achievements over the long term.
- Willingness to effectively use one's training, experience and talents in a business context.
- Uphold, correct or further cultural influences of family, group, ethnic background, current societal trends or economic/physical disadvantage.
- Being able to fulfill personal objectives and achieve long-lasting happiness.
- Capability to create working environment which fosters personal as well as professional growth and becomes a springboard for innovation.

to discover the factors necessary to perform that function, to carry out the function and to evaluate the performance of that activity. All the functions are defined, integrated and furthered by the management actions of section I. At this point, you may begin to feel a bit overwhelmed by the information presented so far in this chapter.

What connection, you might ask, does motivation have with entrepreneurial skills and with small-business talents? Let's answer in reverse. The bulk of this book will be concerned with demonstrating how to use strategic planning to handle the situations requiring small-business talents. The key to successfully do this (at least initially if not throughout the life of the business) is to identify with and use the entrepreneurial abilities and skills described above. But it doesn't mean a tinker's damn to solve business problems with capabilities, insight and the proper attitude unless you are motivated to do so. So, these three exhibits together give the wide and deep picture of what it takes now, tomorrow, next week, next month, next year, and so forth—to get into and stay in business.

At this moment, you may be asking, "Do I have the desire, skills and talents to begin a business career?" Exhibits 3-2 to 3-4 can be used to answer the question. How? One way is to just read them through a few times and then ask yourself, "Am I turned off or on by what I see?" That way works, but not very concretely because it does not let you know why you came to that gut conclusion. A plausible, better way would be to take these three exhibits and evaluate the degree of desire, education and experience for all factors presented for each. Exhibit 3-5 is a template you can use to find out what areas are important, in which you have a key ability and are mature in dealing with. Completing this exhibit and contemplating the results (as shown by example

Exhibit 3-3 Characteristics of Entrepreneurs

I. Qualities. They are:

    A. Self-Motivated. Willing to work long hours to see business succeed.

    B. Persistent. Have perseverance to build a business and see it grow.

    C. Self-Confident. Belief in being masters of their fate. Compete against self-imposed standards.

    D. Self-Reliant. Actively seek situations in which they are personally responsible for success or failure.

    E. Positive yet Realistic. Are optimistic, creative and innovative within recognized limits.

    F. Personable. Get along well with people and are interested in motivating them.

    G. Innovative. Desire to continually respond to changing conditions in creative manner.

    H. Ethical. Abide by consistent, fair and honest guidelines in all business transactions.

II. Skills. They can:

    A. Solve Problems. Consider problems as windows of opportunity rather than barriers to success. Know how to follow through with solution.

    B. Take Risks. Calculate and select those opportunities with moderate risk/reward ratio.

    C. Understand Profit. View as prime indicator of business success, needed to build a business, but not an end in itself.

    D. Set Clear Goals. Direct and plan business activities.

    E. Do Contingency Planning. Develop flexible responses to changing conditions.

    F. Tolerate Ambiguity. Able to live with uncertainty concerning job security and competitor's activities.

III. Characteristics of Entrepreneurs. They:

    A. Learn by Mistakes. Regard failure as a means to better understand a situation and to avoid a similar situation in the future.

    B. Use Feedback. Continually seek information about their work from business associates, customers, professionals, friends, etc. Use the received input to improve business activities.

    C. Communicate. Read, write and speak well.

    D. Develop Outside Interests. Have ways to relax and enjoy leisure to put aside continual business involvement.

Exhibit 3-4 Talents Required for Small-Business People

I. Management

    A. Acknowledge and use array of leadership skills to set and further direction of company.

    B. Understand and implement strategic planning as blueprint to handling all business problems and opportunities.

    C. Realize the techniques and shortcomings of decision making.

    D. Design organization to reflect personalities and skills of firm members and to be responsive to change.

    E. Delimit kinds of control systems and means to effectively implement and monitor their effectiveness.

    F. Establish policies and procedures for implementing the various functional areas (given below).

    G. Evolve a positive and stimulating corporate culture.

    H. Further relations with investors, stockholders, and society.

    I. Guide company growth (rate, product/service mix, new products/services, new companies, acquisition, liquidation, going public, merger, etc.).

    J. Integrate functional activities and outcomes with overall actions.

II. Finance

    A. Concisely define the gamut of financial and accounting factors used. Such factors include (but are not limited to):

        1. Financial ratios (return on investment, earnings per share, equity per share, return on sales, asset turnover, etc.)

        2. Profit

        3. Sales indicators

        4. Functional indicators (inventory cost, production costs, selling cost, hiring and training costs, accounts payable or receivable, R&D cost, etc.)

        5. Company indicators (overhead cost, general and administrative costs, capital requirements, taxes, long-term debt, etc.)

    B. Determine the control system to monitor and evaluate the factors in A.

    C. Describe the kind of tax structure for the business and why it is best suited.

    D. Make decisions about timing, distribution, and sources of capital resources.

III. Marketing

    A. Concisely define the gamut of factors used including (but not limited to):

        1. General economic trends

        2. Competitor products and practices

        3. Product/service line

        4. Advertising and promotion

     5. Market research
     6. Market share(s)
     7. Mix of markets
     8. Pricing scheme(s)
     9. Capabilities for modifying product/service line
    10. Warranties
    11. Credit
  B. Determine the control system to monitor and evaluate the factors in A.

IV. Personnel

  A. Concisely define the gamut of financial and accounting factors used. Such factors include (but are not limited to):
     1. Types of jobs
     2. Kinds of authority required
     3. Communication patterns
     4. Recruiting, hiring, acclimation and advancement methods
     5. Communicate any benefits
     6. Employee participation in management decision making
     7. Firm member incentives
     8. Labor relations and negotiations (where required)
  B. Determine the control system to monitor and evaluate factors in A.
  C. Describe means of improving initiative and innovation.

V. Operations and Research and Development

  A. Concisely define the gamut of factors used, including (but not limited to):
     1. Break-even point
     2. Inventory and ordering methods
     3. Quality of work environment
     4. Production lead time and backlog
     5. Productivity
     6. Quality assurance
     7. Legal concerns (patents, warranties, data rights, guarantees)
     8. Production process, location and layout
     9. R&D support tasks
    10. Distribution channels
    11. Procurement
    12. Insurance
  B. Determine the control system to monitor and evaluate the factors in A.
  C. Describe control system to improve quality of outputs.

Exhibit 3-5 Evaluation of Primary Concerns as You Go into Business (Strength Areas)

Category	Desire			Education				Experience		
	Very Important	Important	Somewhat Important	Strong Ability	Ability	Little Ability	Mature	Some Exposure	Little Exposure	
Motivations (General)										
— Financial Success										
— Own Boss										
— Long-Term Accomplishments										
— Transfer Talents to Business										
— Further Family and Society										
— Fulfill Personal Objectives										
Entrepreneurial Qualities (General)										
— Self-Motivation										
— Persistent										
— Self-Confident										
— Self-Reliant										
— Positive yet Realistic										
— Personable										
— Innovative										
— Ethical										
— Solve Problems										
— Take Risks										
— Understand Profit										
— Set Clear Goals										
— Do Contingency Planning										
— Tolerate Ambiguity										
— Learn by Mistakes										
— Use Feedback										
— Communicate										
— Develop Outside Interests										

Category	Desire			Education			Experience		
	Very Important	Important	Somewhat Important	Strong Ability	Ability	Little Ability	Mature	Some Exposure	Little Exposure
Motivations (General)									
Small-Business Talents									
*Management (General)									
— Leadership									
— Strategic Planning									
— Decision Making									
— Organization Design									
— Control Systems									
— Policies and Procedures									
— Corporate Culture									
— Outside Relations									
— Company Growth									
— Functional/Overall Integration									
Small-Business Talents									
*Finance (General)									
— Factors									
— Control System									
— Tax Structure									
*Marketing (General)									
— Factors									
— Control System									
*Personnel (General)									
— Factors									
— Control System									
*Operations (General)									
— Factors									
— Control System									

Exhibit 3-6 Actual Profile of Business Capabilities (Strength Areas)

Category	Desire			Education				Experience	
	Very Important	Important	Somewhat Important	Strong Ability	Ability	Little Ability	Mature	Some Exposure	Little Exposure
Motivations (General)		+				+		+	
— Financial Success			X			X		X	
— Own Boss	X					X		X	
— Long-Term Accomplishments	X					X			
— Transfer Talents to Business		X				X		X	X
— Further Family and Society	X				X		X		
— Fulfill Personal Objectives		X			X			X	
Entrepreneurial Qualities (General)		+		+				+	
— Self-Motivation	X			X				X	
— Persistent	X				X				
— Self-Confident		X		X			X		X
— Self-Reliant		X		X			X		
— Positive yet Realistic		X			X				
— Personable	X			X			X		X
— Innovative		X				X			
— Ethical	X			X				X	X

Entrepreneurial Qualities (General)									
	+			+	+			+	
— Solve Problems	X	X			X			X	
— Take Risks	X				X			X	
— Understand Profit		X	X		X			X	
— Set Clear Goals	X		X						X
— Do Contingency Planning	X					X			X
— Tolerate Ambiguity			X		X			X	
— Learn by Mistakes	X				X			X	
— Use Feedback	X				X			X	
Small-Business Talents	+			+		+	+		
*Management (General)	+				+		+		
— Leadership	X			X		X			
— Strategic Planning	X			X		X			
— Decision Making	X		X		X	X			
— Organization Design	X					X			
— Control Systems	X				X			X	
— Policies and Procedures		X			X		X		
— Corporate Culture	X			X			X		
— Outside Relations	X			X		X	X		
— Company Growth		X			X		X		
— Functional/Overall Integration		X			X		X		

(continued)

Exhibit 3-6 (Continued)

Category	Desire			Education			Experience		
	Very Important	Important	Somewhat Important	Strong Ability	Ability	Little Ability	Mature	Some Exposure	Little Exposure
*Finance (General)	+			+			+		
— Factors	X						X		
— Control System	X			X	X		X		
— Tax Structure	X			X			X		
*Marketing (General)	+			+			+		
— Factors	X						X		
— Control System	X			X	X		X		
*Personnel (General)	+		+			+			
— Factors	X		X			X			
— Control System	X		X			X			
*Operations (General)	+				+		+		
— Factors	X				X		X		
— Control System	X				X		X		

X - factor indication
+ - category result

in Exhibit 3-6) can lead you to seeing that instead of having only one viable business choice, there may be several alternates to pick from based on your education, experience, and desire.

Next, put these charts aside and jot down all the different kinds of businesses you'd like to be involved with. (Exhibit 3-7 shows several business choices which a would-be entrepreneur considers.) Make the list as long as you would like. Using this brainstorm, mark next to each business choice the strengths and weaknesses for going into it (using Exhibit 3-6). In Exhibit 3-7, include (under the Comments column) the biases toward a particular business (such as a mentor, previous family operation, referral, colleagues in it, etc.). Next, rank your choices by answering these questions:

- Which business(es) do I want to run the most?
- Which business(es) am I qualified to run?
- Which business(es) can best reflect my entrepreneurial characteristics and small-business talents?

A selected sample of businesses and their rankings with justification is shown in Exhibit 3-8. Now, you have the "most likely" list of business prospects. Which of these (or, in some cases, which combination of these) will you choose is based on your best guess for likelihood of success and satisfaction. And, in the end, there is no hard and fast, objective right answer. As Exhibit 3-8 shows, there may be several "equally" promising businesses requiring you to take a risk and make an intuitive selection of the most preferred one. (Further, in chapter 5, we will validate the feasibility of operating the business you chose. If the choice is not workable, another alternative from Exhibit 3-8 would be used.)

Having agreed to which particular business you are to pursue, the final preparatory step to using strategic planning is to define the specific, preferred business. Exhibit 3-9 shows the required parts for a complete definition of your firm. Further, Exhibit 3-10 shows an actual definition for a proposed company. Note that the objectives are directives for the tasks done in the time periods specified. In accomplishing these objectives, the entrepreneur strives to achieve the goals. Generally, several rounds of objectives are carried out to fully satisfy the goals. In addition, the evolution of the business depends on objectives being accomplished, new objectives being defined, goals being reached and sustained, and new goals being strived for. Besides goals and objectives, the mission statements are given.

As will be demonstrated in this book, these statements will play an increasingly important role as the long-term viability of the business comes into view. Also, the purpose is likely to be modified or refined *over* time. If so, explicitly reflect these changes in all parts of the firm's definition.

Exhibit 3-7 Plausible Business Ideas Fitting Exhibit 3-6

Business	Strengths	Weaknesses	Comments

Health Foods Franchise	Enjoy retailing
	Sell products believe in
	Use people skills
	Concern for furthering
	  community
	  awareness
	Obtain financing and
	  training
		Improve management
		  skills
		Improve operations
		  abilities
		Have more exposure
		  solving problems
			Family history

Health Counseling Service	Educated in this area
	Requires little capital,
	  equipment or staff
	Uses people skills
	Uses minimum of
	  financial and
	  management skills
	High degree of
	  innovation
	Improve problem-
	  solving skills
		Community impact is
		  small
		Need to improve
		  innovative and
		  creative qualities
		Lack of long-term
		  commitment to
		  business
			Know several
			others who
			provide this

Cooperative, Natural Foods Bakery	High contribution to
	  community
	Shared business talents
	Obtain personal,
	  professional and
	  group growth
	Further people skills
	High level of ethical
	  commitment
		Learn to have group
		  decision making
		Need very strong
		  planning skills
		Innovation level may
		  drop
		Need to learn and
		  motivate others to
		  fill in knowledge and
		  skills gap
		Commitment can detract
		  from personal life
			Lot of support
			from colleagues

Mail-Order Health Foods	Easily begun out of
	  home
	Interest institutional
	  users to purchase
	Serve wide geographic
	  area
	Need no regular staff
	Small risk of losses
	Working hours and
	  effort completely up
	  to you
		Caution on quality of
		  items
		Large amount of related
		  competition
		Don't really develop an
		  organization
		Doesn't lend itself to
		  long-term growth or
		  innovation	

Business	Strengths	Weaknesses	Comments
Health Foods Inventor	Can be done with financially reasonable resources Have aptitude, persistence and reliance to carry out the invention process Can occur at home alone or with others New products or services can lead to opening related business Can use communication skills to publicize and promote items as well as market patent rights	Large lead time to obtain patents High risk in convincing other firm(s) to make, buy or distribute invented items Long-term gain—need other source(s) of income in the meantime Trade-off between taste, health and shelf life of item	Know three people who own health goods distributorship
Health Foods Spa and Resort	Combine strongest abilities and characteristics and strengthen weaker ones Provide range of goods, services and experiences Obtain maximum use of people skills at many levels Take risk to overcome factors of failure Test ethical practices Make long-term societal contribution	Requires high amount of start-up capital Requires long hours and persistence to succeed Technical skills are fully challenged Essential to do planning and improve skills Lure to make resort your whole life Need form, staff, direct and further effective organization	Know of one for sale

Exhibit 3-8 Ranking of Preferred Business

Business	Ranking	Justification
Health Foods Franchise	2	Correct choice at this stage; yet, dictates of franchisor could be too constraining.
Health Counseling Service	2	High level of people skills; prefer more retail environment.
Cooperative, Natural Foods Bakery	1	Combines the best of my motivations, entrepreneurial characteristics and small-business talents.
Mail-Order Health Foods	3	Could make decent living and enjoy work; however, would like more challenges than see this business providing.
Health Foods Inventor	4	Exciting possibility, but results are too lean in the short term.
Health Foods Spa and Resort	4	Ideal choice if had level of management, resources and capital required now.

Exhibit 3-9 Defining Your Selected Business

I.   Purpose

The statement about the activities which the enterprise will do.

II. Goals

The general statements about the potential achievements of the enterprise.

III. Objectives

The specific statements of the possible achievement for the enterprise targeted to a specific time frame.

IV. Mission

Statements concerning the enterprise's responsibilities to its backers and society.

Exhibit 3-10 Natu-Bake

I. Purpose

To open and successfully operate Natu-Bake, a whole foods, natural bakery specializing in wheat and rice products.

II. Goals

A. To develop a wide variety of nutritious, fresh-baked goods.

B. To provide such baked products at low prices, emphasizing bulk sales and promoting individual purchases.

C. To satisfy the requirements of people on special diets.

D. To produce all goods on a cooperative basis.

E. To expand the product line to include barley and rye products as well as providing hot meal services to institutional food organizations.

III. Objectives

A. To attain sales of $80,000 during the first year of operation.

B. To locate in an area of varied community activities within three months.

C. To obtain all required machinery and initial supplies at least within four months through barter, credit extension and buying used or leasing.

D. To secure seed capital of $50,000 in the next ninety days.

E. To apply and obtain an SBA loan with the seed capital for $180,000, within six months.

IV. Mission

A. To improve the availability, freshness, and nutrition of baked goods for local area residents.

B. To hire members from the community.

C. To participate in community organizing and activities.

D. Each member of the cooperative will give unpaid community service each month.

E. All members are owners.

F. Any volunteer receives a discount on items purchased.

G. To repay any debt within ninety days and any loan within three months of due date.

H. To establish and implement a cadre of ethics and revise it over time.

Chapter 4

Describing Your
Business Life Cycle

SNAPSHOT

Based on the actions of the last chapter, you are ready to begin using strategic planning to solve the problems of making the company go and become a success. True. However, having loaded all the necessary supplies and having checked all the required functions of a ship doesn't mean there exists a well-understood course for the ship to follow.

Likewise, knowing what your business is and the means to solve problems for it doesn't imply that you understand how to achieve longer-term success. Thus this chapter is inserted between picturing your business and the rest of the book to give you something few new business people have—perspective. This chapter will demonstrate a concept you can use for your new business to chart a course for it before you begin operations. The advantage to this is to allow you to have a stronger way of anticipating problems before they occur; that is, to deal with situations before they become crises. The other reason for displaying this "life cycle" concept is to clearly convey the gamut of applications for strategic planning you are likely to be faced with as your firm evolves. Relative to other chapters, this one is short. Yet it is an invaluable portion of starting any business correctly; namely, to see what you are "up against" and what carefully planned actions you will need to take to demonstrate and sustain your firm's competitive advantages.

RECOGNIZING THE FIRM'S LIFE CYCLE

The idea of viewing the changing nature of a business in logical, sequential steps with an integrating concept called "firm evolution" is new. Exhibit 4-1 presents an interpretation of what you can expect to see happen to your firm as time passes

Exhibit 4-1 Stages of a Firm's Evolution

Characteristics	Stages			
	Conception	Initiation	Beginning Operations	Initial Success
1. Strategic Decisions	- Business motivations - Business possibilities	- Items for Influence database - Means of selecting alternatives - Tax structure - Range of outputs - Lawyer and accountant to use - Financing method(s) - Existing or new business - Location	- Unit price(s) - Means of purchasing resources - Computer system	- Client/customer channels - Changes to outputs - Change in location - Overall organizational stratum
2. Major Activities	- Discover entrepreneurial characteristics and small-business talents - Evaluate primary concerns to beginning business	- Identify market segment(s) - Analyze competition - Discover S.W.O.T.[1] - Assess resource requirements - Define control methods and measures	- Define daily operations - Assess need for further financing - Specify gamut of users - Find more ways to penetrate market - Begin advertising and promotion - Discover S.W.O.T.	- Analyze influence Database for information and trends - Refine outputs to increase demand - Rework pricing scheme - Assess need for further financing - Develop guidelines for seeking and using advice - Review strategic planning process - Discover S.W.O.T.

Characteristics	Stages			
	Conception	Initiation	Beginning Operations	Initial Success
3. Structuring of the Organization	- Conceptualize design	- Define basic jobs - Specify particular firm design	- Define hiring and acclimation methods - Establish decision-making methods - Implement modes of communication	- Establish problem-solving procedures - Conduct member evaluations - Depict career advancement pathways - Determine member incentives - Describe functional activities
4. Management Style/ Corporate Culture	- Conceive elements of each	- Describe operational values - Form management concept	- Generate leadership guidelines - Participatory vs. autocratic involvement	- Define organizational culture - Establish a reputation - Define means of handling change

(continued)

Exhibit 4-1 (Continued)

Characteristics	Stages			
	Conception	Initiation	Beginning Operations	Initial Success
5. Accomplishments	- Definition of the firm - Strengths and weaknesses	- Create new organization - Develop initial strategic plan and implement it - Have market penetration scheme - Define means of capital accrual - Delimit primary responsibilities of firm members - Produce business start-up time table - Describe provision method for products or service - Resolve S.W.O.T.	- Discover initial consumer acceptance of outputs - Develop and implement strategic plan - Obtain cost-lean operation - Define plan for growth - Institute management information, budget accounting, and control systems - Finish marketing system - Do contingency planning - Determine initial staffing requirements - Resolve S.W.O.T.	- Delegate authority and distribute responsibility - Develop and implement strategic plan - Sustain consumer base - Achieve financial viability - Attain fluid, yet integrated, organization - Resolve S.W.O.T.

Characteristics	Stages			
	Conception	Initiation	Beginning Operations	Initial Success
6. Controls and Performance	- Compare to existing business	- Planned vs. actual accomplishment - Output level - Output demand fit - Demand level - Capital usage rate - Staff acclimation time	- Unit cost(s) of input(s) and output(s) - Productivity - Demand - Profit margin - People/job fit	- Firm outputs/users match - Management capacity/output match - Return on investment - Productivity rate - User satisfaction - Member satisfaction - Demand rate - Output quality - Information use efficiency - Degree of founder influence - Percent of accounts receivable or payable to total sales - Degree of coping with change
7. Time Frame (months) 2–12		8–24	6–18	8–30

1. Competitive strengths and weaknesses as well as external opportunities and threats.

Exhibit 4-1 (Continued)

Characteristics	Stages		
	Expansion	Crossroads	Maturity and/or Reconception
1. Strategic Decisions	- Additional financing sources - Types and degree of change to organizational structure - Tax structure changes - Going public - Investment opportunities - Trade-offs between short- and long-term success	- Joint venture - Further diversification - Merger - Acquisition - Partial or full-company sale - Buyout - Stabilizing the firm - Bankruptcy - Organizational decline or death - Buying back your company - Franchising	- New goals and objectives - New mission - Kinds of business activities - Mix of leaders/members/innovators - New business operating values - New business sales from public sector
2. Major Activities	- Broaden gain to and from consumers - Refine outputs, their provision and pricing scheme - Upgrade growth plan - Refine support activities - Test and assess contingency plans - Revise influence database - Discover S.W.O.T.	- Rework strategic planning process - Discover appropriate growth rate - Redefine product/service mix and client/customer base - Correct chronic ills - Discover S.W.O.T. - Update controls and control system	- Upgrade means of social responsibility - Respond to competition from former members - Institute "entrepreneurship" - Improve implementation activities - Discover S.W.O.T. - Broaden consumer satisfaction; output quality and markets integration

Characteristics	Stages		
	Expansion	Crossroads	Maturity and/or Reconception
3. Structuring of the Organization	- Enhance member working relationships - Learn from failure - Balance formal vs. informal activities	- Improve structure and work environment - Enhance member career, change four incentive options - Handle member turnover	- Prevent problems using project management - Institute new perspective on training
4. Management Style/ Corporate Culture	- Produce plan for social responsibility - Handle resistance to change - Discover ways of overcoming conflicts	- Refine coporate culture - Redefine founder(s) influence - Plan for leadership succession - Alter management concept	- Rethink advice; giving and receiving - Enlarge leadership capacity - Integrate work style with lifestyle
5. Accomplishments	- Achieve reflective and adaptable organization - Demonstrate effective team and individual leadership - Show ability to handle growth well - Maintain financial viability - Generate high degree of innovation and coordination - Identify and reduce waste - Develop and implement strategic plan - Resolve S.W.O.T.	- Survive as viable organization - Modify set of firm activities - Position firm for longer-term success - Redesign organization - Implement more-effective controls - Develop and implement strategic plan - Resolve S.W.O.T.	- Redefine firm and its structure - Achieve high performance levels - Balance innovation with effective management of current situations - Rekindle entrepreneurial spirit - Develop and implement strategic plan - Resolve S.W.O.T.

(continued)

Exhibit 4-1 (Continued)

Characteristics	Stages		
	Expansion	Crossroads	Maturity and/or Reconception
6. Controls and Performance	- Degree of goals achievement - Percent of market share - Management style/individual leadership match - Effectiveness in handling resistance to change and overcoming conflicts - Change in output quality - Resource use efficiency - Degree of innovation - Soundness of economic and financial ratios - Degree of mission accomplishment - Level of member satisfaction - Level of integrating growth	- Degree of firm solvency - Activities mix/firm definition match - Degree of member adjustment to changes - Effectiveness of firm for long-term survival	- Degree of change response - Diversity of member satisfactions - Degree of problem prevention - Level of long-term viability - Ability to institute improvements - Strength of firm redefinition - Degree of innovation - Improvement in leadership - Work style/lifestyle integration
7. Time Frame (months)	12–36	3–18	3–24

and your efforts and resources used begin to show results. The characteristics specified herein are the common attributes which need be (and usually want to be) considered as the firm progresses. The stages shown here assume that a firm does go from one state of various activities to another state of differing activities.

The assumptions governing Exhibit 4-1 are as follows:

- General Applicability. It can be used for any size firm, any stage(s) of evolution, and any type(s) of business (i.e., new, nonprofit, franchise, etc.).
- Wide Application. The dynamics of evolution are similar in each stage.
- Cumulative Usage. The control and performance measures compound as they move from stage to stage.
- Retention. The results, techniques and insights gained from one stage stay and are used as they move from stage to stage.
- Flexible Pathways. The order of the evolution stage is progressive. Yet, a firm can move forward and back among the stages, or skip over stages.
- Illustrative, not Exhaustive. The elements associated with each characteristic are examples and can be found in stages other than presented.
- Survival Focus. The main thrust of this evolution picture is to demonstrate the firm's continuing existence.
- People Orientation. The emphasis in this graphical representation of a changing firm is on people first, product or service afterward.
- Environmental Dependence. A firm will tend to remain at a particular stage longer if its external and internal environments are stable.
- Transitions. Mechanisms are shown for handling movement from one stage to another.
- Common Tasks. In each stage, develop and implement responses to change, seek feedback from others, obtain pertinent information to make decisions, and formulate and implement a strategic plan.

As these assumptions substantiate, the pattern of evolution of a firm through the stages is dependent on many factors. It is the particular mix of such external and internal factors at points in time which govern the nature of the firm's actions in any stage.

Exhibit 4-1 is the essence of this book. Contained within this chart are the majority of business situations and concerns which must be addressed for a firm to survive, develop and achieve the firm definition (see Exhibit 3-9). This means that Exhibit 4-1 has most of the issues which strategic planning will address as we go through chapter by chapter.

From here on, therefore, the goal is to show how a firm can do well at each stage primarily through the use of strategic planning. That is, strategic planning will be demonstrated multiple times as a key tool to recognize and solve problems in a stage, while at the same time, to prepare the firm to better handle new concerns.

Chapter 5

Initiating Your Firm's Activities

SNAPSHOT

When a new concept is considered by the small business community, it takes groundwork before the concept can be successfully used. This has been the situation thus far. To just "jump in" and immediately use the strategic planning method of chapter 2 would severely dampen the benefits to be gained. Chapters 3 and 4 have provided the well-needed beginning point and framework through which strategic planning can potentially achieve its greatest effects. However, to reiterate, the better your understanding of these previous chapters, the easier, faster and more completely can you apply strategic planning to the burgeoning business situation in front of you. Thus, this chapter communicates how to begin applying the strategic planning method. Particular emphasis is placed on discovering the internal and external influences on your business through starting to build a database of essential information. In addition, the method of strategic planning given in Exhibit 2-1 is harnessed to demonstrate how to address the issues and concerns confronting your business at this stage in a clear, step-by-step and complete manner. As said previously, this stage of the firm's development (like any subsequent stage) builds on the actions and results of the previous stage(s).

ASSEMBLING THE INFLUENCE DATABASE

The major activity done to further this phase of business development is gathering, evaluating and using information. Why? The success of small business is primarily hampered by two factors:

- management inability
- lack of the right kind and usage of information

Management capability and style will be addressed in chapters 7–10. Information is addressed now since it fuels the business activities.

Using the right type of information in a timely fashion for an accurate response to a business situation can be the means of building the firm's success. On the other hand, not being able to obtain the correct information when it's needed to reflect the situation at hand can, over time, be the malady which reduces the potential for full business survival. Thus, as one of the first acts in starting the company, information building must occur.

Sample Task 1

Is the right kind of information ever too costly? How can you ensure that you will not be lacking it? This last paragraph is nothing new to you. these questions arise all the time.

What may be new is the means employed to carry out the information gathering. Basically, there are two kinds of information worth obtaining: external data and internal data. The word *data* is used here to emphasize that the words, numbers, drawings, etc., obtained are initially data. They become information after they are culled, examined and evaluated vis-à-vis the particular concerns requiring them. External data are factors outside the organization which influence the actions of the organization, but which the organization has little or no control over. Exhibit 5-1 shares many of the categories and types of external factors. Exhibit 5-2, on the other hand, shows various sources where such data can be obtained. Much of the data you obtain and use today can quickly become outdated. Thus, in initially sourcing data also make arrangements to receive these media (periodicals, trade publications, journals, reports, printouts, etc.) which can regularly give current and fairly accurate data. There are news and data research services which you can subscribe to (as listed in Exhibit 5-2). Before paying for the service, do a brief "pro-con" evaluation of whether the information eventually derived will be of enough quality and quantity to be worth the cost and cannot be obtained more directly and cheaply.

Internal data factors are displayed in Exhibit 5-3 and sources for obtaining such factors are shown in Exhibit 5-4. These factors are used in a self-appraisal, of (1) the firm's business posture relative to its competition and (2) the firm's overall performance in terms of its strengths and weaknesses. At this point, more information is created by the founders than gotten from other sources. In time, feedback and careful scrutiny of the member's interactions,

Exhibit 5-1 Gamut of External Factors

I. **Economic**
    A. Status of economy
    B. Inflation rate
    C. Interest rate
    D. Level of taxation
    E. Unemployment rate
    F. Rates of exchange
    G. Current balance of payments
    H. Import quotas
    I. Fiscal incentives for commodities
    J. Cost of capital
    K. Capital investment pattern(s)
    L. Credit types and pattern(s)
    M. Change in personal income
    N. Percent of manufacturing capacity
    O. Producer price for finished goods

II. **Social and Political**
    A. Accounting/legal standards and regulations
    B. Population, densities, distribution and mobility
    C. Current consumer buying patterns
    D. Innovations in firm member and public relations
    E. Forces causing social changes
    F. Product disclosure statements
    G. Education levels
    H. Cultural and leisure patterns
    I. Environmental, health and safety, employment, and labor laws
    J. Business philanthropy patterns
    K. Business/community activities and interfaces
    L. Recent legislation
    M. Recent changes in income distribution and age of population
    N. Barriers to market entry
    O. Current aocial attitudes toward business
    P. Current social issues: crime, welfare, abortion, school prayer, advocacy, immigration, deregulations, etc.
    Q. Education and housing patterns
    R. Licenses and fees

III. **Industrial**
    A. Merger acquisition and consolidation pattern
    B. Industry and company profiles

(*continued*)

Exhibit 5-1 (Continued)

C. Data security measures
D. Energy conservation mechanisms
E. Area profiles for location decisions
F. Takeover activities
G. Business creation rates
H. Supply and availability of resources
I. Patent trademark and copyright procedures
J. Contracting with the federal government
K. Methods of doing business abroad
L. Activities and impacts of trade or professional associations
M. Investment patterns of other companies
N. Pricing schemes of competitors
O. Kinds of competitors—by product/service, region and consumer
P. Market shares of competitors—by product/service, region and consumer
Q. Size of market(s)
R. Growth rate of market(s)
S. Diversity and cyclicality of market(s)
T. Current advances in product/service, process or distribution technologies
U. Level of R&D
V. Locational concerns

performance and internal operations will become prevalent (as shown in chapter 7 and following).

Note: The outcome of this data collection procedure is information about events for immediate application. However, as demonstrated in chapter 7, the event-type information is supplemented with trend-type information as the firm ages.

Exhibits 5-1 through 5-4 are comprehensive and are to be referred to often as the firm progresses. Looking at these exhibits now, however, you most likely will ask: What information should I extract first? The answer is to understand your would-be business and your relationship to it. Thus, it is suggested that you create a file on the type of business you want to operate through external written and oral data. Make sure the file has data which can answer all the questions you have prior to starting up the business. In addition do some internal soul-searching to come up with a document stating your capabilities and strengths and potential strengths for running such a business. Include operational values, short-term accomplishments and internal techniques to make the business go and an initial idea of what and how products or services will be offered.

Exhibit 5-2 Sources of External Data

I. Oral discussions with:

    A. Owners and/or operators of businesses with particular emphasis on the type you wish to pursue.

    B. Industry or trade association representatives.

    C. Researchers, professors, lobbyists, and consumers.

    D. Professionals (lawyers, accountants, bankers, venture capitalists, and financial advisors).

    E. Public officials (federal, state, county, local, and international).

    F. Colleagues (friends, family, neighbors, and civic or community organization members).

    G. Information producers (journal/magazine editors, financial analysts, consultants, newspaper reporters, information service firm owners, and radio or TV news analysts).

    H. Technical or operational personnel (engineers, scientists, purchasing agents, insurance agents, computer experts, or suppliers).

II. Written

    A. Newspapers: *Wall Street Journal, USA Today, New York Times*, etc.

    B. Periodicals: Sunday newspapers, *Business Week, Fortune, Time* or *Newsweek*, specific trade or professional periodicals, *Inc., Venture, Working Woman*, etc.

    C. Special reports from associations, conferences or professional meetings, National Technical Information Service (Springfield, Virginia), universities, Congress, individual companies and government agencies (particularly under the Freedom of Information Act).

    D. Websites and books for estimating cost.

    E. Relevant soft- and hard-copy references, such as How to Find Information about Companies, Washington Researchers, Washington, D.C.

Sources of External Data

Washington Information Workbook: The Encyclopedia of Sources, Washington Researchers, Washington, D.C.

International Industry Dossier, Washington Researchers, Washington, D.C.

Company Data Directory, *A Guide to Corporate Filings with the Federal Government*, Washington Researchers, Washington, D.C.

Encyclopedia of Business Information Sources, Paul Wasserman, Gale Research Company, Detroit, Michigan.

A Business Information Guidebook, Oscar Figueroa and Charles Winkler, American Management Association, New York.

FINDEX: The Directory of Market Research Reports, Studies and Surveys, FIND/SVP, New York.

IRS Corporate Financial Ratios, FIND/SVP, New York.

(continued)

Exhibit 5-2 (Continued)

Directory of Industry Data Sources, William A. Benjamin, Gale Research Company, Detroit, Michigan.

International Marketing Handbook and International Marketing Data and Statistics, Gale Research Company, Detroit, Michigan.

The Small Business Sourcebook, John Ganly, Gale Research Company, Detroit, Michigan.

Surveys, Polls, Censuses and Forecasts Directory, Gale Research Company, Detroit, Michigan.

Research Services Directory, Gale Research Company, Detroit, Michigan.

Directory of Incentives for Business Investment and Development in the United States: A State-by-State Guide, The Urban Institute Press, Baltimore, Maryland.

Directory of Online Databases, Cuadra Associates, Inc., Santa Monica, California.

Inc. Magazine's DATABASICS, Doran Howitt and Marvin Weinberger, Garland Publications, New York.

Area Business Databank, Inc., Louisville, Kentucky.

Indices to articles (The Business Periodicals Index, Funk and Scott Index of Corporations and Industries, Facts on File, Wall Street Journal and New York Times Indices, Industrial Arts Index, Congressional Information Index, various technical indices, etc.).

International Listing Service, Tyson's Corner, Virginia (Information on buying/selling businesses and investment opportunities).

Select Information Exchange, New York (Directory of Investment Newsletters).

Hulbert Financial Digest, Washington, D.C.

Mergers, Acquisitions and Divestitures, Thomas Hollis Hopkins, Homewood, Illinois: Dow Jones-Irwin.

How to Profitably Sell or Buy a Company, F. Gordon Douglas, New York, Van Nostrand Reinhold, 1982.

Venture Capital Handbook, David J. Gladstone, Reston, Virginia, Reston Publishing Company, Inc.

Winning Government Contracts, Eli Chappe, Englewood Cliffs, New Jersey, Prentice-Hall.

At this point oral dialogues can yield equal if not better data than written data collections. (Note: No examples are shown here if it is an external data file or internal document because together they are unique to each entrepreneur's beginning pursuit. Given that these items are done, however, the next step can occur completely and quickly.)

SPECIFYING THE KEY STRATEGIC ISSUES

Having compiled an awesome set of data specific to your would-be firms, the next phase in the strategic planning process (Exhibit 2-1) is to articulate the

Exhibit 5-3 Gamut of Internal Factors

A. Organizational
1. Structure
2. Communication patterns
3. Motivation/incentives
4. Decision making
5. Problem solving
6. Corporate culture
7. Leadership
8. Innovation
9. Response to change
10. Ethical business practices
11. Corporate social responsibility
12. Consumerism
13. Control systems
14. Career potential
15. Mix of businesses

B. Performance
1. Growth rate
2. Net profit
3. Break-even point
4. Earnings per share
5. Accounts receivable
6. Sales volume
7. Return on investment
8. Personnel turnover
9. Output per person
10. Resource allocation
11. Firm processes and outputs
12. Marketing activities
13. Firm reputation
14. Information access and use
15. Capital acquisition vs. internal financing
16. Accomplishment of firm definition
17. Effectiveness of strategic planning
18. User satisfaction
19. Ability to handle resistance to change and resolve conflicts
20. Market share
21. Firm long-term solvency
22. Management capacity/output rate match
23. Founder influence
24. Other financial ratios

(continued)

Exhibit 5-3 (Continued)

---

25. Impacts of policies
26. Distribution of capital
27. Market capacity
28. Technical and locational advantages
29. Pricing scheme
30. Output quality
31. Need and type of R&D
32. Inventory turnover
33. Incentive program impacts
34. Degree of risk taking
35. Safety record
36. Position and duration in the industry
37. Level of service quality
38. Sufficient legal protection

Exhibit 5-4 Sources of Internal Data

I.   Written
    A. Previous firm experiences
    B. Policy, procedure, process and control systems
    C. Feedback from consumers, suppliers, competitors, professionals, etc.
    D. Meeting, performance evaluations, strategic planning and task/project records
    E. Documented informal discussions and activities
    F. Internal files and reports
    G. External documents required by law, statute, or charter
    H. Reports/findings from outside consultants
    I. Application of external references to particular internal concerns (i.e., hiring, promotion, automation, layout, financial control, etc.)

II. Oral Discussions
    A. Problem responses
    B. Leisure activity interactions
    C. Informal communications
    D. Firm committees' activities
    E. "Cultural" dialogues (at retreats, seminars, professional gatherings or special occasions—new hire, promotions, holidays, birthdays, terminations, reorganization, ethical adjudication, etc.)
    F. Training sessions

---

strategic issues of concern in this stage of the firm's evolution. Exhibit 5-5 states the major issues of the Initiation Stage (as also shown in Exhibit 4-1). Each question is answered, in turn, by referring to (or updating) the influence (external/internal) database to extract the relevant information for defining various alternatives.

These alternatives are filtered using decision criteria, and preferred causes of actions are chosen. Then using an activity time table, the actions are ordered and done, with minor modifications made as needed. As the action set nears completion, transitions are spelled out to the next stage.

Sample Task 2

How will you verify that your strategic issues at this stage coincide with the ones presented? If your issues do not, what actions will you take? Why?

Each time alternatives are suggested, a choice needs to be made from among them (at this stage or any other). The device used to filter unwanted from desired alternatives is called decision criteria. Exhibit 5-6(A) shows a gamut of decision factors which individually or in combination are applied to the alternatives at hand. A wise and proven technique for making decisions among alternatives is to:

1. first, order the alternatives based on certainty, feasibility and acceptability, for example, from most to least;

Exhibit 5-5 Strategic Issues for the Initiation Stage

- What tax structure is best suited to the firm?
- What is the range of products and/or services to be offered?
- Who will be your potential customers or clients?
- Will the business be new, or will an existing one be bought?
- What location best suits the business at this point?
- Which method(s) of securing financing will be used? Why?
- Who will become the lawyer and accountant for the firm? Why?
- What basic jobs are required now, and what are their responsibilities?
- How will the firm outputs be provided to consumers?
- What is the time table for starting the business?
- What will be the "operational" values used in running the firm?
- What management concept will be invoked, and what firm design(s) are appropriate for this business?
- What are the company's competitive strengths and weaknesses?
- What are the company's external opportunities and threats?
- What are the fundamental control methods and measures to be used?

2. then, use the "filters" of Exhibit 5-6(A) to narrow the choices to a select few;
3. use intuition, nonverbal cues and evolving insights to further refine selected alternatives; and
4. pick alternatives to be carried out.

No decision procedure is fool proof, yet the one given above allows for a flexible combination of objective criteria and subjective perceptions in making the decisions of import to becoming a successful business.

Another equally useful technique for effectively recognizing either strategic issues or strategic alternatives is creativity. Exhibit 5-6(B) demonstrates the steps necessary to successfully make use of creativity in thoroughly handling the concern of interest. The procedure is applied to take the Influence Database and derive from it strategic issues, or to take both of the above and extract alternatives to resolve the strategic issues. Such an activity can be done by a group or by an individual. In any case, the linchpin of creativity is step three: the ability to give enough time off from the effort so previous ideas and perceptions can settle in order to make way for new insights and directions for the concern. Further, the attitude taken during each creative "session" is nonjudgmental. That is, all ideas and causes of action are accepted, and their validity and possible use are explored in an impartial fashion through building on your insights and those of others.

Exhibit 5-6(A) Factors Used to Choose among Alternatives

- Cost to Implement
- Time to Implement
- Member Acceptance
- Consumer Acceptance
- Availability of Resources
- Intensity of Impact
- Duration of Impact
- Ability to Implement
- Previous Successes or Failures with Alternative
- Implement on Limited Basis First
- Return to Status Quo
- Effects on . . .
- Degree of Adaptive Response to External/Internal Change
- Consistency with Firm Definition, Policies and Activities
- Degree of Redundancy, Overlap or Combination with Other Alternatives
- Number and Degree of Restrictions on Current Use
- Number and Degree of Advantages with Current Use

Exhibit 5-6(B) Creativity During the Strategic Planning Process

Steps:

I.   Preparation: Recognition of the concern to be addressed. Agreement on what resources are required, what procedure will be used and which persons will be involved.

II. Clarification: Concern is described in detail, including background, probable causes, attempts at resolution, prior use, impacts of other concerns and on other concerns, and plausible courses of action to be taken now.

III. Gestation: An incubation period follows in which the concern is deliberately not discussed, analyzed or dealt with.

IV. Insight: Flashes of inspiration can occur before the end of the previous step. If not, then return to concern and rethink what its definition is and how to handle it. New relationships or perspectives can emerge herein.

V.   Verification: The arrived-at description of the concern is measured against past experience, collected information and others' ideas to sustain its validity.

VI. Application: The means to take care of the concern are now put into practice.

The use of creativity thus becomes an indispensable part of carrying forth strategic planning.

Using Exhibit 5-5, let's initiate the business. For each strategic issue, the value and significance is discussed, the basic alternatives are shown, and the kinds of decision criteria which, most likely, will be used are given. The actual decision(s) made will, of course, be done by you. But, in the "live" business example pictured later in this chapter, actual decisions are portrayed. The strategic issues requiring response at this point in the firm's development are summarized in Exhibit 5-7 and are described individually below as follows:

A. Tax Structure. Depending on the magnitude of assets, degree of involvement by others and legal requirements, a particular tax structure will be chosen. Variables used to further delineate each alternative are given in Exhibit 5-8. A corporation has all the elements a subchapter S corporation has except that corporations are double-taxed once on their profits and again on the dividends paid to stockholders. In addition, subchapter S corporations may have only one class of stock; no more than 20% of revenue may come from dividends, rents, interest, royalties or stock sales; and may have no more than twenty-five shareholders.

B. Range of Offered Outputs. Some of the characteristics to consider for choosing your "output mix" are given in Exhibit 5-9. Using these characteristics, decisions can occur as to the outputs to furnish (based on Exhibit 5-8).

Exhibit 5-7 Response to Strategic Issues

Strategic Issue	Importance	Alternatives	Decision Criteria
Tax Structure	Defines liability, outside influence and authority of the firm	Sole Proprietorship Partnership/ Cooperative Subchapter S Corporation Corporation	Time to Implement Degree of Adaptive Response Ability to Implement
Range of Offered Outputs	States the major activities of the firm	"High-tech" Products "Lower-tech" Products Standard Services Nonstandard Services Product/Service Mix	Cost and Time to Implement Availability of Resources Implement on Limited Basis
Potential Consumers	Shows where the demand comes from	Individual/Group Organization Income Level Sex/Culture/ Location/Age, Large/Small, Product/ Service Firm	Time and Cost to Implement Duration of Impact Implement on Limited Basis
Business Venture	Specifies how operations will commence	New Existing Franchise	Cost and Time to Implement Availability of Resources Degree of Adaptive Response Effects on Financing, Organizational Design and Type of Marketing
Location	Acknowledges where business will operate	Home Shared Office Space Private Office Space Recycled Commercial Space Other	Cost to Implement Effects on Firm Operations Member Acceptance

Strategic Issue	Importance	Alternatives	Decision Criteria
Financing	Provides "lifeblood" to firm operations	Equity—Short or Long Term Debt—Short or Long Term Equity/Debt Mix	Time to Implement Degree of Recurrence Degree of Adaptive Response
Professional Services	Gives advice to assisting with smooth operations	Lawyer Accountant Other	Cost to Implement Member Acceptance Degree of Adaptive Response
Required Jobs	Defines basic responsibilities	Technical Administrative Mix	Time to Implement Ability to Implement Implement on Limited Basis
Firm Outputs' Provisions	Delineates means to sell outputs	Retail Wholesale Direct Mail Special Contract Combination	Cost to Implement Implement on Limited Basis Effects on Distribution Channels
Time Table	Gives firm blueprint for coordinating start-up activities	PERT/CFM GANTT Milestone Other	Cost to Implement Time to Implement Ability to Implement
Operating Values	Demonstrates sensitivity of founders to sustaining positive actions	Financial Communication Quality	Member Acceptance Ability to Implement Degree of Adaptive Response

(continued)

Exhibit 5-7 (Continued)

Strategic Issue	Importance	Alternatives	Decision Criteria
Management Concepts	Shows perspective used in dealing with people, problems and future	Reactive Proactive Interactive	Time to Implement Ability to Implement Degree of Adaptive Response
Firm Design	Sketches the kind of organization desired	Functional Geographic Output Consumer Matrix Lattice Hybrid	Time and Cost to Implement Member Acceptance Degree of Adaptive Response
Competitive Strengths and Weaknesses	Demonstrates ability to be successful in the marketplace	Leadership Social Responsibility Innovation Motivation/Challenge	Intensity of Impact Effects on Marketplace Degree of Adaptive Response
External Opportunities and Threats	Shows effects of marketplace on operations	Competitor Outputs Consumer Behavior Political/Technical/ Social Events Economic Indicators	Intensity of Impact Effects on Internal Operations Degree of Adaptive Response
Control Methods	Describes procedures for upgrading proficiency of firm operations	Inspection Testing Positive or Negative Incentives Combination	Cost and Time to Implement Implement on Limited Basis Degree of Adaptive Response

Exhibit 5-8 Alternative Tax Structures

Characteristics	Tax Structures		
	Sole Proprietorship	*Partnership*	*Subchapter S Corporation*
Start-Up Procedure	Registration with State and Begin	Agreement, State Registration, and Begin	Incorporate with State and Charter
Liability	Unlimited	Unlimited	Limited to Anoint of Stockholder Investment
Profit Sharing	All to Owner	Partners	Stockholders
Continuity	Depends on Owners	Depends on Partners	Transfer of Stock
Modifications	Directly by Founder	Done by Partner Consensus	Done by Board of Directors Approval
Taxes	Personal	Personal	Personal
Legal Restrictions	Few	Few	Several
Capital Acquisition	Small, Informal	Small, Varied	Large, Varied

    C. Potential Consumers. As with Range of Offered Outputs, some concerns to use in deciding on who your target purchasers will be are given in Exhibit 5-10.

Sample Task 3

What is more important to specify—kinds of products and/or services, potential clients, or customers? Why?

    D. Business Venture. The decision to start afresh, purchase an existing firm or become a franchise is based on many concerns. A few of these are shown in Exhibit 5-11. The bottom line (as discussed in Exhibit 5-7) is what value each type of venture has versus the start-up costs to operate it. A franchise can generally be said to have high start-up costs and high value. New or existing businesses are more variable. As shown later, a careful demarcation of what initial capital is required as well as how much control flexibility is possible is crucial to making this decision.

Exhibit 5-9 Characteristics of Offered Outputs

- Types: simple, complex; unique, well-known; personal, professional; tangible, intangible; cheap, costly
- Frequency: one time, periodically, continuously
- Variety: one, many; products and services
- Quality: unique, well-known
- Amount of Control: small, large
- Timeliness: response to crisis or fad, long-term usage
- Provision: given alone, given with other outputs
- Changes: easily done, difficultly done
- Payment: individual, group sale; single, multiple contracts
- Competition: shallow, stiff
- Application: one, many; seasonal, year-round
- Break-even Point: short term, longer term

Exhibit 5-10 Characteristics of Potential Consumers

- Buyer: individual, group, organization
- Individual: man, woman; young, older; wealthy, less wealthy; ethnic, mainstream; urban, rural; home, apartment; single, married; educated, less educated; blue, white collar; local, national; few interests, many interests
- Group: homogeneous, heterogeneous; small, large; close-knit, loose; short affiliation, long affiliation
- Organization: small, large; local, national, international; public, private, institutional; technical, nontechnical; general, specific needs

E. Location. This aspect varies tremendously by business type. It may be of little or no concern to an on-site security consultant or of tantamount importance to a gas station owner. In either case, thinking through what the current or projected location decisions are likely to be (see Exhibits 5-12 and 5-7) is of high value.

F. Financing. There are more avenues open to secure initial capital for your business today then ever before. Using Exhibit 5-13, decide which combination of sources will give you the capital you require. Consider whether the financing is
- long or short term
- secure or nonsecure
- equity or debt preferred
- first, second, etc., round of financing
- large or small amount (as percent of current or projected revenue)

Exhibit 5-11 Characteristics of a Business Venture

Characteristics	Business Venture		
	New	*Existing*	*Franchise*
Unique Output	Appropriate	Nonexistent	Nonexistent
Standard Output	No. Operate uniquely	Yes. Structure and market in place	Yes. Financing, structure and market in place
High Competition	High risk	Moderate risk	Low risk
Existing Operation and Policy Problems	No constraints	Current restraints	Proven general effectiveness in handling concerns
Decision Making	Your own	Assume existing operations	Directed by franchiser
Start-up Concerns	Many	Few	Few
Transition Concerns	None	Many	Few
Resource Requirements	Many	Several	Few
Direction Setting	Wide Open	Constrained	Restricted
Reputation	Unknown	Variable	Basically sound

Exhibit 5-12 Factors Considered in Locating a Business

- Proximity to Consumers
- Proximity to Support Personnel (accountant, lawyer, suppliers, wholesalers, distributors, brokers, etc.)
- Closeness to Means of Production (facilities, plant, warehouse, hospital, mine, dock, etc.)
- Importance at This Time
- Availability of Resources and Special Supplies
- Safety, Security, and Environmental Concerns
- Zoning Regulations and Other Ordinances
- Surrounding Development Pattern

Exhibit 5-13 Various Methods of Securing Financing

I. **Equity Capital. Contributor obtains share of business profits and decision-making influence.**
   A. Founder
   B. Savings from Friends, Relatives or Colleagues
   C. Informal Investors (i.e., doctors, lawyers, engineers and small-business people)
   D. "Seed" Capitalists (successful business people and financiers)
   E. Venture Capitalists
   F. Foundation or Pension Funds
   G. Large Company
   H. Investment Banker
   I. Stock Issuance
   J. Merger, Acquisition or Joint Venture

II. **Debt Capital. Contributor loans money with payback period and interest rate predetermined.**
   A. Financial Institutions (bank, S&L, mortgage company, finance company, and insurance company)
   B. Brokerage House
   C. Private Corporation
   D. Credit Union
   E. Friend, Relative or Informal Lender
   F. Fraternal Organizations
   G. Cooperatives
   H. Government Agency (federal, state or local)
   I. Small Business Investment Company
   J. Pension Funds
   K. Universities
   L. Association for Small Business Advancement
   M. Owner of Existing Business

Also, wise strategic planning would have you specifying when, where and how much capital you might require over the next two to five years.

G. Professional Services. These are provided by outside advisors or experts on an as-needed bases to resolve concerns in an unbiased, timely and transferable manner (see Exhibit 5-14).

These autonomous individuals work closely with the firm members and operations to provide accurate recommendations for specific actions. Yet you are the final decision-maker (as shown in Exhibit 5-7) and continued user of the insights, procedures or solutions provided. The key to using a lawyer, accountant or consultant is not to rely on her

Exhibit 5-14 Attributes of Professionals

- Provide objective, unbiased analyses of your concerns
- Use on regular basis to bring you current perspectives on legal, accounting and other matters
- Perform significant tasks to keeping the business going (audits, adjudication, legal conformance, raising capital, taxes, expansion, liaison with public officials and private parties, etc.)
- Solve critical problems on request
- Lend credibility to successful operations
- Assist with contracts, insurance and changes in tax structure
- Have proven track record, credentials and references for proper selection
- Work with on contract—with terms and tasks clearly delineated
- Subject to periodic evaluation and switch to others
- Can supplement your staff in providing expertise at generally less cost than per-member expense

to keep reinventing the actions required to take care of the concern in question, but to internalize those actions in dealing with future, similar concerns.

Sample Task 4

Demonstrate how you can start a business without conferring with a lawyer, accountant, or consultant. Is this your preference? Why?

H. Required Jobs. Exhibit 5-15 gives the design guidelines for delineating "who should do what with whom" in the beginning. In many cases, the firm founders are likely to do the majority of the jobs. Yet, this exhibit is to stimulate thinking and action of why, how and when the responsibilities and tools should be further divided and delegated to the growing number of nonfounder members. The objective (as reflected in Exhibit 5-7) is to accomplish the largest number of activities with the fewest and most competent persons.

I. Firm Outputs Provisions. Once the product or service is developed, how will it reach the potential consumer? Exhibit 5-16 gives the variables to consider in distributing the end item. Tangible goods are likely to require "middle persons" to prepare and match them with other goods together to be channeled to specified users.

Also, they will need storage, one or more transshipments, material handling and varied delivery schedules. Services, by contrast, are

Exhibit 5-15 Features of Required Jobs

- Basic Tasks
- Direct Responsibilities
- Decision-Making Authority
- Influence with and from Founders
- Means of Executing Control
- Career Growth Potential
- Relationships to Other Required Jobs
- Amount of Training or Retraining Required

generally provided directly to users with little warehousing or handling required, Yet, delivery terms can be as complex as with products. Again, the decision alternative for Exhibit 5-16 is Exhibit 5-7.

J. Time Table. This tool is an invaluable means of portraying the activities to be done, their priority, accomplishment date and interface. Any technique mentioned in Exhibit 5-7 should, if properly executed, show the strategic issue decisions and their consequences, including:
- the content and order
- timing
- effects on other decisions
- implementation schedule

Exhibit 5-17 demonstrates the design criteria for formulating and using the decision time table.

K. Operating Values. This topic was first discussed in Exhibit 3-3. However, this presentation was to "test" whether you have what it takes to begin and sustain a business. Exhibit 5-18 is a list of those insights and acts which you want to see become part of the everyday challenge and fun of running the business. This list should be used in conjunction with Exhibit 5-7 to discover which values are to be incorporated with which basic firm functions. In doing so, the tone and direction for the working environment will be set.

L. Management Concepts. The literature is overflowing with various versions of the "management concept." The reason for including it at this juncture is simply to note that the founder would try to accomplish everything alone if possible. There are other resources which can provide valuable insight, actions and support to the entrepreneur. These "resources" are the other firm members who in working with you, growing with you, and learning by mistakes as you do can become more adept at running the business with suggested future actions and

Exhibit 5-16 Means to Providing Firm Outputs

I. **Distribution Channels**
   A. Direct
   B. Indirect—one or more intermediaries

II. **Transportation Options**
   A. Ground
   B. Air
   C. Domestic and/or Foreign

III. **Transshipments**
   A. One
   B. Several

IV. **Storage Space**
   A. Large, Small
   B. General, Special
   C. Long, Short Term

V. **Materials Handling**
   A. Little, Lot
   B. Special, General
   C. Intermittently, Frequently

VI. **Delivery Terms**
   A. Deliveries: one, many
   B. Payment: before, after
   C. Location: one, many
   D. Time: rarely, frequently
   E. Size: large, small

objectives. In addition, they can give the support required for the entire company to chart new courses of actions and undertake additional business endeavors (see Exhibit 5-19).

Sample Task 5

Assume that you initiate the business without articulating what your operational values or management concept are. Are there any problems which may occur "down the road" as a consequence of this?

Exhibit 5-17 Time Table Features

I. **Means of Display**
    A. Manual
    B. Automated

II. **Frequency of Update**
    A. Weekly
    B. Monthly

III. **Ease of Corrections and Additions**
     A. Interactive
     B. Off-line

IV. **Interrelationships and Overlap of Firm Activities**
    A. Shown on Time Table
    B. Developed Separately

V. **Access**
    A. Restricted
    B. Unrestricted

VI. **Usefulness**
    A. Done in any Business Evolution Stage
    B. Display Firm Evolution

Exhibit 5-18 Operating Values

- Aesthetics
- Order
- Humor
- Congeniality
- Comfort
- Fairness
- Clarity
- Completeness
- Performance
- Flexibility
- Enjoyability
- Personal and Firm Growth
- Listening
- Self-Reliance
- Compatibility
- Consistency and Continuity
- Perseverance
- etc.

Exhibit 5-19 Elements of a Management Concept

- Orientation
  Toward Change, Away from Status Quo
- Direction
  Toward Achievement and Risk-Taking, Away from Order and Security
- Decision Making
  Based on Particular Situation, Not on Canned Technique
- Relationships
  Toward Interactive, Participatory and Equal, Away from Reactive, Mandated and Unequal
- Delegation
  Toward Better Mix of Personalities and Positions, Away from Arbitrary Responsibility Distribution
- Planning
  Toward Problem Prevention, Away from Problem Solving
- Control
  Toward Maximum Self-Control, Away from Imposed Corporate Controls
- Aspirations
  Toward Greater Personal Growth and Organization Fulfillment, Away from Higher Prestige and Status

M. Firm Design. Most organizations begin helter skelter and evolve like Topsy. This time the situation can be different. By pinpointing the "building blocks" of an organization (see Exhibit 5-20) you can pick and choose the attributes (and their demarcations) which reflect your design concept for the firm. Then placing them together can cause the organization structure to emerge (as shown in chapter 7).

N. Competitive Strengths and Weaknesses. Based on the internal data (of Exhibit 5-3) and the other strategic issues given, a summary of the firm's ability to compete is generated. These pluses and minuses of the firm are specific and are shown later in the strategic plan for the initiation stage.

O. External Opportunities and Threats. Based on the external data and strategic issues, a picture of the forces propelling and constraining the firm in the marketplace is given. As with the internal strengths and weaknesses, these insights are specific to a particular business and thus are shown in the strategic plan following.

P. Control Methods. Control is a process in which organizational activities are evaluated and improved through performance review.
  It is a crucial element in sustaining and improving the quality of the firm actions and interfaces. As Exhibit 5-21 demonstrates, control aids in the movement from one stage to the next in the firm's evolution. The

Exhibit 5-20 Firm Design Components

A. Division of Labor
   1. Generalists
   2. Specialists
B. Communication Modes
   1. Interpersonal
   2. Team
C. Distribution of Authority by
   1. Position
   2. Performance in Tasks
D. Functions of Message Flow
   1. Inform
   2. Instruct
   3. Persuade
   4. Command
E. Responsibility (for goal setting, decision making or strategic planning)
   1. Held
   2. Shared
F. Incentives
   1. Basic or Extended
   2. Dictated or Shared
G. Corporate Culture
   1. Refined and Formal
   2. Flexible and Informal
H. Coordination
   1. Promulgated by Founders
   2. Determined by Members
I. Motivation
   1. Organizationally Driven
   2. Group or Self-Driven
J. Resistance to Change
   1. Low
   2. High
K. Work Climate
   1. Maintenance
   2. Innovation
L. Span of Control
   1. High
   2. Low
M. Departmentalization
   1. Service or Product
   2. Client or Customer
   3. Functional
   4. Geographic

　　　5. Matrix
　　　6. Lattice
　　　7. Hybrid
　　　8. Other
　　　9. None
　N. Structure
　　　1. Formal and Fixed
　　　2. Informal and Flexible
　O. Control
　　　1. Directed from the Top
　　　2. Self or Group
　P. Relationship to Firm Definition
　　　1. Close
　　　2. Loose

---

methods of control shown in Exhibit 5-7 have general application in all aspects of firm operations, including personnel, finance, production, distribution, marketing, response to change, and strategic planning. Exhibit 5-22 lists possible measures of control for use during this stage (and subsequently as well).

Having seen the gamut of strategic issues, their characteristics and some general alternatives to resolve them, the next step is to demonstrate the strategic plan for a business in the initiation stage. Exhibit 5-23 shows what the contents of this plan should be, with Exhibit 5-24 depicting how feedback would be elicited about the plan. To reiterate, the results from implementing the plan will be a prelude to the next stage.

STRATEGIC PLAN IN ACTION

To properly and effectively initiate a business, strategic planning is essential. To further sustain this point, Exhibit 5-25 shows the definition for Coplan's School of Dance. This business will provide instruction and training to male and female youths, ages five to eighteen. The founder, Elizabeth Coplan, comes out of the work world in wanting to combine her hobby, education and past experience in a small business that will go. (Exhibit 5-26 presents her resume.) Next, following the strategic planning framework, an influence database is established.

Sample elements for it are shown on Exhibit 5-27. A wise idea is to begin collecting articles on trends in dance instruction, dance schools and dance school management. In addition, Ms. Coplan surveyed the local area

Exhibit 5-21 Characteristics of Control

I.   Method
   A. Set performance standards
   B. Observe actual performance
   C. Compare actual to standard performance using a technique
   D. If deviations occur, either:
      1. Correct actual performance
      2. Change standards
      3. Both 1. and 2.
      4. Do nothing since the actual performance exceeds the standard(s)

II.   Techniques
   A. Inspection: Examine design attributes of the output(s) for quality level. Examples
      of inspection standards include:
      1. Thickness
      2. Smoothness
      3. Logic
      4. Format
      5. Temperature-Resistance
      6. Completeness
      7. Uniqueness
      8. Interchangeable Components
   B. Testing: Determine the operational attributes of the output(s) for quality level.
      Examples of testing standards include:
      1. Noise
      2. Accuracy
      3. Failure rate
      4. Number of applications
      5. Uniqueness
      6. Tolerance limits
      7. Response time
      8. Efficiency

Exhibit 5-22 Control Measures in the Initiation Stage

- Planned versus actual accomplishment
- Output level
- Demand level
- Output/demand fit
- Capital usage rate
- Staff acclimation time
- Marketing indicators

Exhibit 5-23 Strategic Plan for the Initiation Stage Elements

I.   Firm Definition

II. Influence Database

III. Strategic Issues and Alternatives
   A. Tax Structure
   B. Characteristics of Offered Outputs
   C. Potential Consumers
   D. Types of Business Ventures
   E. Business Location Considerations
   F. Financing Methods
   G. Using Professional Services
   H. Required Jobs
   I. Firm Outputs' Provisions
   J. Start-Up Timetable
   K. Operating Values
   L. Management Concept
   M. Firm Design
   N. Competitive Strengths and Weaknesses
   O. External Opportunities and Threats
   P. Control Measures

IV. Decision Criteria

V.   Selection of Alternatives

VI. Implementation of Alternatives
   A. Time Table
   B. Summary of Positive and Negative Attributes

VII. Monitoring
   A. Feedback
   B. Control Methods

VIII. Appendix
   Cash Forecast

Exhibit 5-24 Obtaining Feedback

- Source of Feedback
- Reasons for Asking for Feedback
- Overall Impressions of Strategic Plan
- Strengths of Plan
- Weaknesses with Plan
- Specific Tasks to Improve Business Design
- Resources—People, Money or Material to Obtain
- Strategic Issues Needing Additional Emphasis
- Date of Feedback Session

Exhibit 5-25 Presenting Coplan's School of Dance

I. **Purpose**. To provide the local community with an innovative, service-oriented establishment to instruct students between the ages of five and eighteen in the basic principles of classical ballet, modern jazz, tap and dance dynamics.

II. **Goals**
   A. To create an exciting learning atmosphere for students of dance.
   B. To provide a wide assortment of dance activities.
   C. To develop and improve teaching techniques which will ensure highest quality of instruction.
   D. To encourage input, feedback and innovation from all firm members.
   E. To reach a large and diverse community of youth and adults with small-group instruction.
   F. To market the dance business and instruction concept to other communities.

III. **Objectives**
   A. To attain sales of $55,900 by the end of the first year of operation.
   B. To locate in a familiar area with a high potential demand for dance instruction within three months.
   C. To provide dance instruction and supplies to students upon opening the studio.
   D. To secure $25,000 in seed capital in the next ninety days.
   E. To open doors for instruction within two months of obtaining capital requirements.

IV. **Mission**
   A. To better the way dance is taught to children and young adults.
   B. To stimulate more creative and constructive activities among youth in the chosen community.
   C. Later, to offer special services for the handicapped.
   D. To have staff who work and live in the community.
   E. To encourage active participation of members, students and parents in community functions.
   F. To donate space, instruction demonstrations and money to augment targeted community activities.
   G. All members will share in financial success of firm.
   H. To provide dance instruction in return for administrative support.

Exhibit 5-26 Qualifying the Founder

Elizabeth A. Coplin
400 W. 29th Street, S.E.
Washington, D.C. 20002
(202) 888-4111

Past Experience

A. 9/08–present. Administrative Assistant, The Cobbs Institute, Washington, D.C.
In charge of coordinating all seminars, meetings, conferences and special events. Arranges space, provides speakers, obtains entertainment, does all expenditures and accounting, hires part-time staff, and compiles information for marketing efforts and annual report.

B. 7/07–8/08. Insurance Broker, The Safeguard Consortium, Washington, D.C.
Responsible for sales of domestic insurance to working women or men in a three-county region. Was number-one salesperson-of-the-month three times. Assisted with developing new, joint work/home insurance based on customer feedback.

Education

2003. Bachelor of Business Administration, with major in Marketing, University of the District of Columbia.

2000. Certificate of License, Broker of Insurance, Washington, D.C.

Talents

1999–present. Part-time dance instructor, Sills Dance Academy, Suitland, Maryland.

1995–1999. Part-time dance instructor, HIE-Top Studio, Washington, D.C.

1990–present. Performer and choreographer, various local dance concerts.

Entrepreneurial Aspirations

My work experience, education and my love for dance have all engendered a sense of what my own business could be. I come from a family history of sole proprietors and thus feel that I have the drive to be one with my "own kind". My commitment is to my work at this point in my life. I desire my work and my hobby to be the same.

In addition, knowing how dance schools are run, I am positive that mine could successfully compete in quality of instruction and number of students served.

Will I put in whatever time it takes to make the School of Dance successful? Unquestionably. Further, my perspective is to engender a working environment where all participants are giving and receiving, learning and communicating so that the reason for being is realized sooner rather than later. Finally, to guide the initial success, growth and maturing of the School of Dance, strategic planning will be learned and practiced by all.

Personal:
Age—42
Health—Excellent
Marital Status—Single

Exhibit 5-27 Setting Up the Influence Database

Category	Item	References	Use	Impacts
External	*Samples*:			
	Location	Past experience Realtors Business colleagues	Decide on place	Affect demand and customer service
	Competitors	Past experience Yellow pages Dance professionals	Orient business	Determine path to initial success
	Consumer Interest	Founder Survey Discussions with parents, teachers, and students	Gage degree of interest	Scale initial size of operation
Internal	*Samples*:			
	Structure of Organization	Articles Colleagues Members	Management by walking around	Shows how individual will relate and work
	Marketing Activities	Competitors Similar firms Trade associations	Define how demand will be generated	Regulate number and rate of consumers
	Controls	Members Colleagues Experts	Regulate how services are provided	Service improvement, higher productivity and expansion opportunities

and found that there are four well-known dance schools. She profiled each school to find its enrollment per week, charge per class, hours of operation, age group served, number of instructors, wage rates and additional activities. (These will be discussed in the next chapter when compared with Coplan's daily operations.)

After compiling the pertinent data, strategic issues and alternatives can be next addressed. Using Exhibits 5-5 and 5-23 to identify the strategic issues and Exhibits 5-6(A) and 5-7 to choose viable alternatives to deal with these issues, Exhibit 5-28 gives a summary of the important concerns for initiating Coplan's School of Dance. Being a sole proprietor appears the simplest and quickest way to begin operations since the firm's liability is small. The kinds of classes offered are both unique and well-known, can be taken on a regular basis or at special, one-time workshops, reflect dance principles which are used to instruct in other dance courses (beyond what are given here), can be modified without difficulty, are taught year-round and together can help obtain a break-even point early in the firm's operations. Most students signing up for classes are individuals, not groups. The Coplan School of Dance is a new business founded to provide greater flexibility and quality in dance instruction.

The possible location for the business is a shopping center since the space available is usable, close to public transportation, convenient for parental shopping while their kids are in class, and near schools, churches, libraries, and community recreation centers, several housing and apartment developments and across from new housing being built. Further, the space is zoned for this kind of commercial use, is 1,050 square feet and costs about $91.50 per square foot per year (the going commercial rate in shopping malls in this region). The space will require renovation to be divided into three instruction rooms (one 20' x 20' and two 10' x 15'), a foyer/office area (12' x 15'), a bathroom and small storage area. The space will be leased on a five-year basis. Elizabeth Coplan will put up $30,000 of her money and is seeking a $250,000 SBA commercial loan (at 10% interest over thirty years). After considering several options, she has decided to retain a lawyer and accountant to facilitate the start-up (each one knows the other and can provide "team" service).

Sample Task 6

What if the SBA loan does not come through for the dance studio? What suggestions can you give of alternative financing channels which Elizabeth should explore as contingencies?

Exhibit 5-28 Strategic Issues for the Initiation Stage of Coplan's School of Dance

Issue	Strategic Alternative(s)	Reasons	Comments
Tax Structure	Sole Proprietorship	Easiest and least costly to implement	
Outputs	Classical ballet, modem jazz, tap and dance dynamics classes	• No more costly to have one or four different classes • Create high degree of consumer acceptance	
Consumers	Youth of varying age, sex, and dance experience	• Founder's ability is with youth • Consistent with firm definition	Appeal to individuals
Business Venture	New	• Constraints to opening are small • Have skills to provide outputs better than existing firms	Work with lawyer and accountant to set up
Business Location	Close to consumers and other services— in shopping center	• Cost-effective • Resources are available • Consumers and firm members will accept • Growing area • Many advantages	
Securing Financing	Personal savings plus SBA loan	• Have prerequisites • Done successfully by other firms	
Professional Services	• Preferred Attorney • Preferred Accountant	• Understanding of this business • Reputation	

Issue	Strategic Alternative(s)	Reasons	Comments
Required Jobs	Senior Dance Instructor Junior Dance Instructor Secretary/ Receptionist	• Basic skills needed to effectively serve consumers • Persons are available with these skills • Selected persons can be tried on limited basis	
Outputs' Provisions			Not relevant since service given at point of purchase
Time Table	Done at each stage	• Ease of making corrections • Use to reflect adaptive responses to change	
Operating Values	Congeniality Enjoyment Listening Clarity	• Affect students' performance and satisfaction • Affect public relations with parents and community • Affect interaction among members and building firm spirit	
Management Concepts	Learning to adapt to change	• Affect long-term quality and survival of firm • Consistent with firm definition	

(*continued*)

Exhibit 5-28 (Continued)

Issue	Strategic Alternative(s)	Reasons	Comments
Firm Design	Open, flexible and evolved through participation	• For long-term impacts • Out of experience with other dance schools • For highest degree of member acceptance	
Competitive Strengths and Weaknesses	+ High-quality classes + High degree of variety and frequency of classes + Sound reputation of founder + Solid backgrounds of instructors - Members have not worked together before - SBA loan may not be approved - Lease for space may not occur - Scheduling concerns	• Affect ability to operate dance school initially	
External Opportunities and Threats	+ Serving community need + Stimulate other business activity in selling dance clothes and shoes + Create barter with other firms in shopping center - Demand may not occur - Responses by existing dance studios to lure students away	• Impact ability to implement strategic plan • Affect short-term firm survival	

Issue	Strategic Alternative(s)	Reasons	Comments
Control Measures (Samples)	• Number of students served per week • Teaching hours per week • Number of inquiries per week	• Affect on meeting expenses, instructor satisfaction demand increase	• To be used at next stage

The major tasks to be done are instructing in dance and office administration, typing, reception, and some bookkeeping. Ms. Coplan will serve as senior instructor and hire a part-time junior instructor and office administrator/secretary. Both firm members should have prior experience in dance instruction and office managing, respectively. The time table to get the operations started is presented in Exhibit 5-29. The thrust of this organization is to provide a working environment where all members contribute to daily operations, decisions, success and problem solving. The satisfaction is derived as much from what one does as how one structures the tasks. Guidance from the founder is given as suggestions and insights rather than as procedure and dogma. The "bugs" to be worked out as the firm begins include the ability of everyone to be compatible, effectively allocate their work time and make enough money to see profits being made. On the other hand, building community rapport and expanding the business activity needs to be tempered with a lagging demand or the competitor's response to the existence of a new firm. Finally, the cash forecasts of Exhibit 5-30 will be used to secure the loan. The assumptions behind the chart (as discussed further in the next chapter) are

- Revenue. Have thirty-two hours per week of operation with forty-three hours of classes. Each student pays $50 per hour of instruction. Months 1 and 2 assume have four students per class; months 3 to 5 assume have five students per class; months 6 to 12 assume have six students per class. Also, each new student pay an annual registration fee. This fee is offset by special discounts discussed in the next chapter.
- Salaries. Senior Instructor teaches twenty-five hours per week at $70/hour. Junior Instructor teaches eighteen hours per week at $50/hour. Secretary/Office Manager works twenty hours per week at $60/hour.
- Payroll Expense. Ten percent of salaries.
- Benefits. Health, life and disability insurance. Also, instructors have profit-sharing of 66% and 34% respectively.

Exhibit 5-29 Time Table to Begin Operations

Activity	Time frame					
	Month 1	Month 2	Month 3 ...	Month 7	Month 8	Month 9
Do Strategic Planning	————————					
Seek Professional Services	————————					
Determine Financing Requirement		————				
Seek SBA Loan			———————			
Locate Site				————		
Commence Marketing				—————————		
Secure Loan					*	
Renovate Space						————
Purchase and Install Equipment						————
Hire and Acclimate Staff						————
Begin Operations						*

Exhibit 5-30 Cash Forecast

I.	**Fixed Costs**		

Item			Expenditure
A.	Renovation of Location Space (including security system)	$	5,500
B.	Furniture (including typewriter and floor pads)		1,800
C.	Dance Equipment		1,700
	1. Rails and Mirrors		900
	2. Stereo System		300
	3. Tapes and Records		500
D.	Licenses, Security Deposit and Initial Supplier Payments		2,500
E.	Preopening Promotion		1,000
F.	Contingency Expenditures		2,000
G.	Total	$	14,500

II. Variable Costs and Forecast (see next page).

(*continued*)

- Rent. Assume 1,050 sqare feet at $91.50 per square foot per year.
- Insurance. For liability to outsiders or damage.
- Taxes. Assume 35% tax bracket.

The controls and means of solving issues for the school at this stage are sketched in Exhibits 5-31 and 5-32. The "comment" column in Exhibit 5-32 (as with comparable exhibits in subsequent chapters) is to make special reference to implementation conditions.

Further, when this plan is implemented, the objectives of Exhibit 5-25 are sought for accomplishment. Assuming that Coplan's School of Dance does satisfy them, then as prelude to the next stage, new objectives would be formulated. Such objectives might include the following:

- To raise $250,000 of reserve capital in the next six months
- To charge 5% less than all competitors for equivalent dance instruction within ninety days
- To obtain and retain 15% of the youth dance market within one year
- To ensure that average costs per item or activity are reduced 10% annually for each of the next three years

Exhibit 5-30 (Continued)

Line Item	Month 1	Month 2	Month 3	Month 4	Month 5	Month 6	Month 7	Month 8	Month 9	Month 10	Month 11	Month 12	Total
I. Revenue	3,440	3,440	4,300	4,300	4,300	5,160	5,160	5,160	5,160	5,160	5,160	5,160	55,900
II. Expenses													
A. Salaries	1,540	1,540	1,540	1,540	1,540	1,540	1,540	1,540	1,540	1,540	1,540	1,540	18,480
B. Payroll Expense	154	154	154	154	154	154	154	154	154	154	154	154	1,840
C. Benefits	133	150	150	150	150	150	150	150	130	150	150	150	1,800
D. Supplies													
E. Advertising	500	250	250	250	100	100	100	100	100	100	100	100	2,050
F. Accounting & Legal Fees	875	—	—	—	—	200	—	—	—	—	—	405	1,480
G. Rent	800	800	800	800	800	800	800	800	800	800	800	800	9,600
H. Telephone	60	60	60	60	60	60	60	60	60	60	60	60	720
I. Utilities	80	80	80	80	70	70	70	70	70	80	80	80	910
J. Insurance	150	150	150	150	150	150	150	150	150	150	150	190	1,800
K. Depreciation	40	40	40	40	40	40	40	40	40	40	40	40	-440
L. Maintenance	30	30	30	30	30	30	30	30	30	30	30	30	350
M. Loan Payment	200	200	200	200	200	200	200	200	200	200	200	200	2,400
N. Photocopy Rental	115	115	115	115	115	115	115	115	115				
O. Petty Cash	200	200	200	200	200	200	200	200	200	200	200	200	2,400
III. Total Expenses	4,894	3,769	3,769	3,769	3,618	3,819	3,619	3,619	3,619	3,619	3,619	4,024	44,780
IV. Gross Profit	(1,454)	(329)	531	531	681	1,341	1,541	1,541	1,541	1,541	1,541	1,136	11,120
V. Taxes			185.85	185.85	238.35	469.35	539.35	539.35	539.35	539.35	539.35	397.60	3,892
VI. Net Profit			345.15	345.15	442.65	871.65	1001.65	1001.65	1001.65	1001.65	1001.65	738.40	7,228

Exhibit 5-31 Using Controls in the Initiation Stage

Control	Measure	Standard	Data Input	Interpretation
Planned versus actual accomplishment	Actual time divided by planned time for any activity	1.1	Activity records	If doing a task takes 10% or more time than planned, further scrutiny is needed
Output level	Number of dance class hours per week divided by operation	70%	Scheduling records	At least 70% of all operating hours be devoted to dance classes
Demand level	Actual students divided by planned students	0.9	Activity records	If student number is 10% or less than planned, further scrutiny is needed
Output/demand fit	Number of dance classes divided by total number of students	6	Scheduling and registration records	At least six students be enrolled in each class
Capital usage rate	Dollars spent per week divided by total dollars available to spend	0.8	Financial records	No more than 80% of funds should be used each week
Staff acclimation time	Actual acclimation time divided by planned	1.2	Personnel survey	If it takes 20% or more additional time for member to adjust above what is planned, counteraction need be taken
Marketing indicators	Number of inquiries per week divided by total number of different classes offered	0.8	Marketing and scheduling records	Inquiries should run at 80% or more of class offerings if demand is to grow

Chapter 5

Exhibit 5-32 Response to S.W.O.T.[1]

S.W.O.T.	Point of Discovery	Possible Response	Comment
Member Cohesiveness	Initial concern	• Have acclimation method • Provide periodic gripe sessions among members • Hold retreats to build member skills and strengthen attitude	
Initial Financing	SBA loan	• Allocate funds wisely • Have contingency funding sources • Ensure repayment schedule	
Space Leasing	Site for studio	• Have alternate sites chosen • Have alternate renting arrangements • Consider purchasing space	
Scheduling	Primary activity	• Develop system and test it • Review schedule periodically • Have schedule reflect demand	
Barter	Discussions with reciprocal firms	• Do not do it • Find many firms to have arrangement with • Limit dollar amount of barter per firm • Select firms based on strategic value outputs to dance school	
Lack of Demand	Registration records and telephone inquiries	• Increase promotional efforts • Reduce prices • Target specific market segments in more depth • Seek new consumer groups	
Competition's Responses	Marketing literature from other firms	• Wait and see • Counter moves with better promotion, dance activities, prices, etc. • Hold special dance events to retain existing clientele	

[1]Competitive strengths and weaknesses and external opportunities and threats.

- To test and verify all contingency plans within six months
- To define and agree on means to grow by 20% annually within the next nine months
- In addition, all results and techniques learned at this stage will be updated and reapplied in subsequent stages.

Finally, from Exhibits 5-31 and 5-32, the demand for classes has not materialized as planned and the staff hired is taking longer to acclimate than the standard calls for. These two factors will thus be carried over as unresolved strategic issues in the new strategic plan. In addition, the facts that the business is established in location, financing and operations leads to a reformulated strategic plan whose orientation is toward building an organization balanced between people and process activities.

Chapter 6

Beginning Your
Firm's Operations

SNAPSHOT

Many new business people carry out the activities described in the last chapter. They define their business, discover the initial problems to be solved, and create a plan to solve these problems and get money to continue. Once this "plan" is completed and the financing is secured, the plan, in many cases, becomes dusty, and is revived only when new monies are sought. That is why this is a critical chapter in the book. It aptly demonstrates why planning cannot cease as the "doors open," how modifying the plan to reflect the next set of strategic issues can directly focus the firm's energies and resources and what additional advantages are gained by continuing to do strategic planning. The information used in describing the strategic issues discussed below comes from the compiled influence database of the last chapter.

DELINEATING THE STRATEGIC
ISSUES FOR BEGINNING OPERATIONS

Once the transition is completed from the last stage new challenges and obstacles begin to crop up as signs of evolution. These concerns are dealt with using the strategic planning process (Exhibit 2-1) and the decision criteria of Exhibit 5-6(A). In brief, the opportunities and threats, strengths and opportunities which the firm members are likely to face at this stage are listed in Exhibit 6-1. Each of these will be explained in turn in a separate exhibit and/ or in the update of the strategic plan shown in Exhibit 5-23.

Exhibit 6-1 Strategic Issues for the Beginning Operations Stage

- What daily operations are to be carried out?
- What additional financing requirements exist?
- Who are the length and breadth of users for our outputs?
- What unit price will be charged for our outputs?
- How will the market be further penetrated?
- What kind of advertising and promotion program will be used?
- How will input resources be purchased?
- Which hiring and acclimation method(s) will be chosen?
- How will decisions be made?
- What modes of communication will be tried?
- What are the guidelines governing leadership?
- How will costs be kept down?
- What growth plan will be chosen?
- Which M.I.S., budgeting and accounting systems will be used?
- What contingency plans need be developed?
- Which computer system will be selected?
- How will the current strategic plan be reformulated?
- Which competitive strengths and weaknesses are important for this stage?
- Which external opportunities and threats are important for this stage?
- How will control measures be defined and applied at this stage?

Sample Task 1

How quickly can you start your business and achieve financial success? Oh, what is the rush? Might you lose some valuable experience required for long-term survival along the way?

A. Daily Operations. This strategic issue is to answer the question of what functions can be done on a daily basis or in a day's time. Exhibit 6-2 gives important food for thought about how to structure the operations. One common mistake made in beginning operations is to brainstorm a way of doing business and be so pleased with the effort of conceptualizing a complete method that no refinement of the method occurs. This chart gives you the planning opportunity to hone the method to reduce problems later.

B. Additional Capital. There is an old adage that goes something like this: if business is your game, then money becomes your middle name.
The "chronic" need for more financing is an ever-present issue with growing companies. So the real concern is not whether to obtain additional capital, but when and how. As with the other graphics, Exhibit 6-3 gives guidance to practically considering the magnitude of money, the timing of funding sources, and the frequency of receiving funds. In addition, thought is directed to plan for future money needs.

Exhibit 6-2 Anatomy of Daily Operations

I. Functional Components
    A. Finance
    B. Marketing
    C. Production
    D. Management
    E. Other

II. Types of Activities
    A. Simple
    B. Complex
    C. Routine
    D. Unique

III. Input Requirements
    A. One or Many
    B. None—one or more functions
       accomplished first

IV. Output Requirements
    A. Completed or Intermediate
       Function
    B. One or Many
    C. Impacts none, one or more
       functions

V. Process Varieties
    A. Simple or Complex
    B. Manual or Automated
    C. Good or Service Oriented
    D. Single or Multiple

VI. Operation Frequency
    A. Per hour
    B. Per 1/2 day
    C. Per day

VII. Operation Variability
    A. Similar tomorrow
    B. Somewhat different tomorrow
    C. Totally different tomorrow

VIII. Operation History
    A. New and incomplete
    B. Stable and developed
    C. Secure and predictable

IX. Method of Operation
    A. Fixed
    B. Varies with inputs and/or process

X. Change to Operation
    A. Done easily
    B. Done with difficulty

Exhibit 6-3 Is There a Need for More Capital?

- First, determine current net expenditures per month.
- Next, compute increase or decrease in net monthly expenditures during subsequent twelve months.
- Specify amount budgeted for working capital over the next year.
- Specify amount of revenue expected per month.
- If the difference between revenue plus capital and expenditures is getting smaller or is negative, then:
  - Consider short-term means to reduce expenditures
  - Delineate sources for "second round" financing
  - Estimate magnitude of capital required with justification
  - Articulate optional entry techniques for approaching sources
    = One or more sources?
    = Debt capital only, equity capital only or a mixture?
    = General or specialized institutions?
    = Short- or long-term arrangement?
- If capital is not required now, when might it be and what should be done to obtain it?

C. Full Description of Consumers. Based on Exhibit 5-10, now a complete characterization of those purchases and users of your outputs is done. This information can be voluminous, sophisticated and expensively procured or it can be brief, pertinent and readily applicable. The key concern in using Exhibit 6-4 is to ask, what are the end uses of the customer or client profile you create? The answer to this question will direct how much energy and expense will be put into gathering and evaluating this background marketing data.

Sample Task 2

How would you profile your potential consumer? What needs of his or hers are you filling? Describe three major needs you could also fill by showing how your existing resources and operations could handle them. Might you later expand your outputs to the public?

D. Output Price. To know what price to charge for each product or service, three things must be known:
- The qualities and variations of the outputs
- Competitor(s) price(s)
- The cost of each output

With these data inputs, you can then focus on formulating the pricing scheme. As Exhibit 6-5 depicts and Exhibit 7-6 describes, each pricing situation is tailored to the present cost, competition and consumer situations.

Sample Task 3

Brainstorm five different pricing schemes for your product(s) and/or service(s). Rank the order the schemes. What ranking criteria did you use? When will you use each pricing scheme? Why?

Exhibit 6-4 Complete Base of Customers or Clients

- Geographic Range: single or multiple areas, local or regional, rural or urban
- Buyer Characteristics: gender, age, ethnic bent, education or income level, marital status, individual, group or organization
- Buying Habits: often; one or new or repeat etc., in person, at a distance; cash, credit; seldom, several locations; preshopping, direct buying, buying; at home, office or store; alone, in a group
- Sources of Customers/Clients: competitors, referrals, association membership lists, yellow pages, professional/civic gatherings, direct advertising or promotion, consumer lists, etc.

Exhibit 6-5 Price for the Output(s)

Considerations
- Similar or different outputs
- Narrow or wide variation in output features (size, shape, color, timing, versatility, weight, multiple uses, accuracy, long-lasting, etc.)
- Production or service cost
- Prices for equivalent competitor items
- Prices for similar output(s) you provide
- Single price or price scale
- Price scheme (discounts, bonus and special circumstances)
- Profit percent of the price
- Other factors (credit, insurance, storage, delivery or packing charges)

E. Consumer Market Penetration. What you are attempting to accomplish here is the same as with the outputs: namely, to find that "mix of ingredients" which will stimulate demand. Some market penetration "ingredients" are given in Exhibit 6-6. Those are put into practice in this stage and reviewed for improvement in Exhibit 7-5.

F. Advertising and Promotion Methods. No means for penetrating the marketplace with your goods and/or services is complete without these tools. The thrust in Exhibit 6-7 is to stimulate the use of your outputs and thus generate more sales. Yet, whether advertising or promotion are used alone or in combination, the bottom line is not increased revenue, but greater "item awareness" through word-of-mouth referrals which then can lead to more sales.

Exhibit 6-6 Ways to Further Penetrate a Consumer Market

Concerns
- Level of market entry now
- Assessment of market penetration schemes
  - Acknowledgement of effective methods with reasons
  - Acknowledgement of ineffective methods with reasons
  - Selection of altered set of methods to broaden influence on market
- Means to reach more consumers:
  - Media spots
  - Human interest articles in major newspapers and magazines
  - Product or service awards
  - Tailoring outreach to each market segment of interest
  - Joint advertising or promotion with other outputs
  - etc.

Exhibit 6-7 Advertising and Promotion Methods

Technique	Resources
Brochure	Direct Mail Lists
	Associations
	Consumer Firm Lists
Announcement	Newspaper
	Magazine
	Journal/Trade Publication
	Newsletter
	Public Places (buildings, transit, billboards, etc.)
	Yellow Pages
Commercial	Radio
	Television
Telephone Solicitation	Phone Book
	Professional Membership
	Consumer List

Type	Media
Short, written pieces on related topic	Newsletter, journal, magazine, trade publication or newspaper
Longer, written pieces	Publisher, journal, newsletter, trade periodical or newspaper
Giveaway or discount	Direct mail or in person
Listing	Membership directory or business directory
Short oral presentation	Professional meeting, public forum, conference, TV, or radio
Longer oral presentation	Advocacy hearing, regulatory meeting and college course

Sample Task 4

Create a schedule for when you would use advertising and when you would use promotion. At what times in starting your business would you use only one type? At what times would you use neither? Why?

G. Purchasing. Whether simple or complex, large or small, frequent or infrequent, any business needs to buy things. Most small business owners assume there are more important activities than this to do, and thus relegate purchasing to a done-as-required category. Exhibit 6-8 shows that when lack of attention is paid, a purchase can end up with higher cost, lower quality, untimely and troublesome items. Instead, spending a focused session to find the smart ways of ordering items, procuring goods or services and buying to special requirements can make a sizeable difference in your ability to deliver the outputs for your customers or clients.

H. Hiring and Acclimation Methods. At this point in the firm's growth, energy is spent on defining the jobs of the business, now and in the foreseeable future. Once the tools to be accomplished to further and maintain the growth are understood, then matching these tools with the abilities, education, experience and attitude of individuals occurs. Exhibit 6-9(A) demonstrates how to effectively locate, screen, interview and evaluate prospective candidates to do the above jobs. The key is to believe in your new members and they in the new venture, when all other considerations are settled. Many small companies hire new members and "let them attain their buoyancy level" on their own. Sadly, the mistake here is failure to effectively nurture the achievement capability of new members.

Exhibit 6-9(B) says nonsense to this shortcoming and instead provides a way for the member to adjust and adopt to the new business environment—a way which will keep returning benefits to the other members and the individual.

Exhibit 6-8 Purchasing of Resources

Factors
- Type, quality and amount required
- Frequency and constancy of purchase
- Special concerns including availability, delivery, schedule, handling, and inventory levels
- Purchasing mechanisms
  - Wholesale or retail
  - Cash or credit
  - Direct mail vs. personal contact
  - Customized vs. standardized ordering
  - Purchasing agent vs. direct buying
  - Lease or buy
  - Barter vs. cash
  - Produce or buy
- Selection of suppliers
  - Reputation of suppliers
  - Source of referral
  - Reasonableness of bid
  - Discounts, services and quality extras
- Inspection and receipt of goods

Exhibit 6-9(A) Action Sheet for Recruiting

Preparation
1. Determine job design for positions required, including:
   • Qualifications (experience, education, and special skills)
   • Responsibilities
   • Career advancement
   • Compensation and benefits
2. Advertise career opportunities through:
   • Word of mouth
   • Professional journals
   • Newspapers
   • Recruiting agencies
3. Screen resumes based on job design criteria.
4. Also, screen part-time, summer, or work/study employees for possible candidates.
5. Choose candidates and schedule interviews.
6. Decide on interview procedure and whether interviews conducted by individuals, group, or both.

Interview
1. Coordinate discussions to avoid repetition and to discover various aspects of candidates' personalities and abilities.
2. Help candidates feel "at home."
3. Develop a checklist for all information needed from candidate and how it will be obtained.
4. Allow candidate to initiate discussion.
5. Define evaluation method and use consistently for every interviewee.

Action Sheet for Recruiting
Hiring
1. Determine leading candidates and talk further with each one.
2. Gather and synthesize impressions from colleagues.
3. Check candidate's professional references.
4. Rank candidates and make decisions through consensus.
Either:
5a. Make offer to candidate. Receive acceptance or make other offer.
Finally, hire new firm member.
or
5b. Recruit further or cease activity.

Exhibit 6-9(B) Action Sheet for Acclimation of New Members

First Day

1. Greetings and Welcome
   - Visits with one or more founders
   - Meets firm members
   - Assigned a staff colleague to help with acclimation
2. Given Information Briefing
   - Firm history
   - Operating philosophy
   - Expected contributions
   - Advancement guidelines
   - Evaluation and review
   - Training and job satisfaction
   - Professional activities
   - Summary
3. Completes Benefits Forms
   - Fills out tax, insurance, and health forms
   - Chooses benefits package

First Week

1. Participates in company seminar
2. Discovers area of responsibility
3. Meets colleagues who will be working with and for

First Month

1. Establishes professional relationship(s) with consumers, suppliers, etc.
2. Develops rapport with colleagues
3. Produces first results on project
4. Participates in training (specifically, in strategic planning and other skill building) as well as extracurricular activities

First Year

1. Completes one or more assignments
2. Has one or more peer evaluation sessions
3. Further rapport with colleagues
4. Suggests and implements improvements to company operations
5. Accomplishes one or more objectives toward career advancement
6. Does one or more personal assessments about future with company

Sample Task 5

Figure out how long it would take you to thoroughly hire and acclimate new members compared to hiring new employees. Is the time difference cost-effective? Why?

I. Decision Making

The most important management activity the members of any firm does is to solve problems. This is particularly true for new businesses. A part of business problem solving is decision making. There are hundreds of ways given to make a decision, but only one method completely works—and that is to state the alternative ways of handling a problem situation and to choose those you will use.

Exhibit 6-10 cogently presents how decision making is used to solve problems. Also, it shows that an effective solution to one problem can help solve others and prevent future problems. Thus, all members of the firm should be familiar with this method. Also, observations are in order:

• indecision can be worse than a decision because you are giving up any direct opportunity to direct or control.

Exhibit 6-10 Elements for Making Decisions

• Generally, for a problem situation
  - State the problem(s)
  - List the causes for each problem
  - Describe how problems overlap or affect each other
• Need delineate alternatives to resolve problem or problem set
  - Brainstorm wide variety of alternatives—quantitative and qualitative
  - Obtain input from several sources
  - Ensure sufficient number of options
• Articulate choice mechanism
  - Use decision criteria (see Exhibit 5-6(A))
  - Apply criteria to alternatives one or several times until obtain smaller, preferred set of alternatives
  - Prioritize implementation of chosen set
• Specify implementation actions
  - State means of carrying out each alternative
  - Give way of monitoring and evaluating implementation
  - Discover time frame and resources needed to complete implementation
• Find transitions to future problem concerns
  - Notice how problem solutions assist with defining and resolving other problems
  - Use solutions as means to prevent future occurrences where possible

---

- decisions made under negative circumstances end up with less than positive results.
- timing is key—rank decisions and consider interactive impacts.

J. Communication Modes. No business is transacted, no accomplishments are made and no furtherance toward achieving firm goals occurs without communication. What each group of members comprising an emerging organization discovers is how to communicate so that the above activities will happen. Usually such discovery happens without forethought or sensitivity to the communications problems which can arise early and stay late into the firm's development. And, usually most firms have communication difficulties with their members, suppliers, consumers, competitors, etc. Is it the normal course of firm progress that people will not be able to communicate well with each other? Exhibit 6-11 shows an approach to communication which can be used from the beginning to sensitize firm members to what kind of communication is needed in the situation at hand. That is, people can choose to communicate differently (and better) in different situations and contexts, with different people. This exhibit means that firm members will need to practice finding and using the various communication modes in order to improve their basic communication. Beyond this, it is not always possible to choose the correct mode for each communication instance due to the large number of variables affecting communication. That is, such factors as nonverbal gestures, timing, receptivity, environmental distractions, level of trust or credibility, time pressure, bias, inability to listen, and so forth affects how one person or group attempts to convey information to another person or group. However, to deal with these factors and, therefore, enhance the chance for successful communication, you can do the following:

- repeat the message to clarify it
- use simple language not laden with jargon
- think through beforehand what you wish to say
- verify timing and receptivity
- ask for feedback
- find a suitable location
- ensure actions support and are consistent with communications
- establish trust
- become more aware of nonverbal gestures, eye contact, and interruptions and context

Together, Exhibit 6-11 and the above suggestions give you a blueprint for sustaining improved communication skills.

Exhibit 6-11 Modes of Communication

I. Communication Inputs

  A. Type of Communication
   1. Passive—empathetic. Listens and acknowledges understanding from other person
   2. Passive—rational. Views, listens and records activities
   3. Active—empathetic. Presents and clarifies actions for other person to do
   4. Active—rational. Presents ideas for other person to consider

  B. Degree of Control
   1. Total control. Communicator directs all interaction
   2. Shared control. Communicator and other person vacillate between larger and smaller amounts of control
   3. No control. Other person directs all interaction

  C. Precipitating Factor—situation requiring communication attention
   Examples:
   1. Resistance to change
   2. Conflict
   3. Information gathering
   4. Policy clarification
   5. Chronic concern
   6. New venture
   7. Modified strategic plan

II. Communication Outputs

Modes of Communication

Modes	Type of Communication	Applications
A. Acceptance	Passive-empathetic	Explaining issue situation Discussion with other person's supervisor Personal problem or opportunity
B. Observation	Passive-rational	Collecting data Recording performance of implementation plan Assessing communication during a meeting
C. Motivation	Active-rational	Providing alternatives to resolve a problem Concisely defining an issue Presenting a means for follow-up and feedback
D. Confrontation	Active-empathetic	Redesign organizational structure Lay off key member Correct unethical practices
E. Persuasion	Active-empathetic	Review future actions to keep problem resolved Change to a noncredit operation Have findings validated by a third party

Sample Task 6

Try out these suggestions and Exhibit 6-11. What do you notice after one day, three days, one week, two weeks, one month, and so forth? Has learning to communicate made a difference in how you do business?

K. Leadership Guidelines. Start with the operational values of Exhibit 5-18. Add in the management concept of Exhibit 5-19. Synthesize these together and use Exhibit 6-12 to then handle situations as they occur to direct the energies and resources of the firm. Effective leadership means member and leader satisfaction with resolution of the situation, now and later. As is stated in this exhibit, leaders change, situations change and so leadership must evolve to reflect those changes. The blueprint pictured here emphasizes that the opportunity for good leadership exists with each new situation.

Realizing the positive leadership potential comes from the way the aforementioned exhibits are combined and applied.

L. Cost Reduction. Earlier we discussed obtaining capital. The thrust there is to find what monies you need when you need them with a

Exhibit 6-12 Guidelines for Leadership

Precepts
- All firm members can assume leadership responsibilities
- Leadership is learned and furthered by doing
- Ways in which leadership is accomplished include: individual, group and inter group; formal or informal; and with much or little resistance
- Bottom line of leadership is to achieve objectives and later goals of the organization
- Leadership has no general application; instead, is directed to specific situations at hand
- Leadership is a creative mix of skills (communication, knowledge, experience, insight, respect, patience, tact, charisma and ability to motivate) oriented differently to each situation

Practical Pointers
- Understand specific concerns requiring leadership
- Ascertain what leadership qualities are required to handle the concern
- Determine if you are the "right" person to lead
  - If not, suggest who should direct the resolution of this concern
  - If so, develop beforehand several approaches to dealing with the concern
- Obtain feedback on the approaches
- Achieve consensus on approach(es) to be taken with members impacted by results
- Implement, closely monitor and reinforce approach(es) used

minimum number of conditions attached. Once the money is gotten, smart entrepreneurs use it the same way—namely, they spend money for what's required using efficient and timely channels and by incurring a minimum number of negative side effects. Exhibit 6-13 and the small business example below show how you can have least-cost operations with high levels of activity, amenities and quality.

M. Growth Definition. Once a business concern has all the vital ingredients, the next step would be to put them together so that what the firm does it can:

- continue to do
- do better
- do in larger amounts
- do in other ways

Exhibit 6-14 shows the major concerns to consider in perceiving the kind, amount, timing and alternatives for growth. As the live business situation demonstrates, making growth work means thinking it through early.

N. Information and Control Systems. The backbone of any modern small business is to access, use and change information. The way to ensure the information is accurate, timely and applicable is through control (as shown in Exhibit 5-21). Now, Exhibit 6-15 sketches the assumptions

---

Exhibit 6-13 Ways to Reduce Costs

Operating Principles

- Any cost activity can be decreased; there is a trade-off between quality of results and expenditure to obtain them.
- For each new cost task, assess cost factors to obtain several ways of accomplishing activity. Choose least costly means of fully completing task.
- Assess whether various tasks should be combined and the impact between cost efficiency and task effectiveness.

Practical Pointers

- Always find out more than one cost for accomplishing the same end.
- Develop consistent procedures for defining and keeping track of costs.
- Have regular, periodic assessment of the cost of items and services required to support the business. Make any necessary revisions.
- Develop adequate and accurate record-keeping to validate expenditures and flag areas for cost improvement.
- Do income projection for the next time period and strive to actually incur less than budgeted costs or understand how to do so for the next time frame.
- Recognize that reducing costs is done similarly for purchased items as for internal labor and materials.

---

and actions required to define and decide on how to monitor and improve the generation and application of information.

Without such a system of information retrieval, control and monitoring the firm will face unexpected problems frequently and will miss unexpected opportunities.

O. Contingency Planning. Most businesses, large and small, operate by finding a pattern, sticking to that pattern and making changes only when "forced to." This statement holds true for successful or unsuccessful businesses. When asked about contingency situations (as shown in Exhibit 6-16) most business persons respond that they are highly unlikely, are handled by insurance, delegated to the lawyer or accountant or do not really matter. Further, when asked if contingencies are good or bad, most entrepreneurs associate them with crises or emergencies. In fact both assertions are, at best, half true. Contingencies are, by definition, not everyday occurrences. But the impact of any such occurrence is large. Most impacts of contingencies are negative,

Exhibit 6-14 Defining a Growth Plan

I. Strategic Variables
   A. Current Activities
   B. New Activities
   C. Quality
   D. Performance

II. Strategic Issues and Alternatives
   A. What rate of growth is desirable?
   B. When should growth occur?
   C. How will growth happen?
   D. What impacts are anticipated from the growth chosen?
   E. What contingencies need to be taken into account?

III. Decision Criteria
   A. Ability to try growth alternative on limited basis first
   B. Compatibility with operational philosophy
   C. Time to implement
   D. Resources and people
   E. Previous successes or failure with alternative

IV. Implementation
   A. Control measures to monitor growth
   B. Growth vs. achievement at this stage—match or mismatch?
   C. Effects on influence database

Exhibit 6-15 Discovering Which Information and Control System to Use

Given:
- Database framework with sources of data, means of sifting important information from them, and applications toward strengthening.
- Responses to internal and external problems.
- Need to order all accounting and budgeting data in an easily understood, comprehensive and accurate framework tailored to the specific business.
- The policy of consistently, frequently and thoroughly reexamining the usefulness, timeliness and reliability of control data used to monitor and direct most firm activities.

Then:
- Generate several alternate, automated solutions.
- Choose one or more alternatives based on breadth of users, flexible features, ease of interaction and error correction and format of outputs.
- Use chosen system(s) to define information requirements depending on:
  - Position in company
  - Time of the month or week
  - Interface with others
  - New insights or information recently obtained
  - Problems or opportunities at hand
- If system(s) do not meet your short or longer-term needs, make changes to modified or new system(s) expeditiously.

Exhibit 6-16 Contingency Planning

I.   Definitions
  A. Contingency: an event, situation or set of actions which prevents an organization from achieving its objectives. Such events or situations occur in an unforeseen manner.
  B. Contingency Planning: the recognition and preparation for such occurrences by asking "what if" questions and designing responses for them. The developed plans are placed in readiness in case such situations should arise.

II.   Contingency Occurrences
  A. Singular crisis event: requires immediate or short-term response. Usually such an event cannot be predicted or sought after. (Example: Tylenol scandal in 1980s)
  B. Evolving trend: situation appears after certain threshold is exceeded. Such outcomes are usually unnoticed or not considered. (Example: Foundation crumbling)
  C. Uncalculated changes (either external or internal) directly affecting the implementation of strategic alternatives. (Example: Member disclosing trade secrets)

III. Categories of Contingencies

	Examples
A. Physical	Fire, flood, earthquake, machine failure, power outage, vandalism, bomb, threat, lightning, robbery, hurricane, personal injury, product defect, etc.

B.	Economic	Sudden change in financial ratios, productivity, reputation, personnel, product quality, material or capital supply, etc.; takeover threat; extra normal investment gains or losses; product or service recall; or sudden increase or decline in competitors' activities
C.	New Technological Breakthrough	Laser, VCR, digital music disc, etc.
D.	Human	Death or sudden resignation of firm founder, customer/client boycott, strike, change in member performance
E.	Political/Regulatory	Unexpected rule-making, abrupt foreign changes, change in leadership

IV. Formulating Contingency Plan

Define situations which could occur and what kind of responses are appropriate. Use plans to eliminate fumbling, uncertainty, confusion and time delays in reacting to unexpected events. Steps to a contingency plan include:

A. Purpose and Trigger Mechanism(s). What conditions are likely to put contingency plan into action, and what strategic issues (problems or opportunities) need to be addressed?

B. Impacts of contingency on operations

C. Ways to mitigate (or exploit) impacts

D. Procedure to resolve impacts (including redundancy as things such as interlock, double-shield, etc.) where required

E. Control mechanisms and modification of contingency plan to fit specific occurrence

F. Relationships of outcomes to strategic planning

V. Other Observations

A. Whenever possible, do test or dry run of each contingency plan, if possible, under varying circumstances

B. Ensure various contingency plans are not conflicting

C. Review and update contingency plan(s) periodically to ascertain whether:
   1. Continued relevance and usefulness; if no, discard
   2. Proper trigger mechanisms are being used
   3. Contingency plan(s) can effectively handle current contingencies
   4. There is a need for additional plans
   5. Can incorporate contingency plan(s) or results as part of strategic planning. One instance to do so is when trigger mechanism(s) become well enough understood and predictable to be included in "Influence Database" (see Exhibits 5-1 and 5-3)

NOTE: Contingency plans are developed for situations of high risk with low probability of occurring. The bottom line is to have the fewest number which effectively address those issues deemed outside the strategic planning process. Over time, incorporate more and more contingency plans within strategic plans.

but not all. Thus, there is a method in Exhibit 6-16 for ascertaining what the magnitude and various effects of any contingency is likely to be in advance and to prepare for dealing with it to either:

- minimize the destructive impact, or
- turn the impact to your advantage

The response to any contingency will be part quality control and part public relations. Further, how does a contingency plan work?

Answer: it is well thought out, tested, and has firm members participate in learning how to use it. In fact, the objective here is to incorporate as many contingencies within strategic planning as is feasible. Why? So that when carrying out the chosen strategic alternatives, "what if" questions can be asked in case the alternatives must be modified, corrected or oriented to new opportunities. In fact, Exhibit 6-16 gives guidance to change and shows when a contingency plan needs to be changed. The greater the importance or risk of any contingency, the more closely the plan's usefulness will be monitored.

Sample Task 7

Name three contingencies you could face in the near future. How will your "gut" tell you to handle them? How can you better the "gut level" response using the information herein?

P. Computer System Selection. There is so much advice, courses, and sources and other information on this topic that one could be overwhelmed by it. Nonetheless, to cut through the information overload, Exhibit 6-17 shows an effective means of obtaining the computer system which is well-matched to your needs. Following this suggested scheme means first defining what your current and projected need will be and then discovering the software/hardware (in that order) mix to satisfy these needs. Because, if you select a system with a half-aware idea of your computer applications, the garbage-in, garbage-out syndrome will decide what the system will be like.

Q. Strategic Plan Reformulation. No strategic planning process is complete without creating a subsequent strategic plan. One method of accomplishing this task is presented in Exhibit 6-18. The reformulation begins when most, if not all, the strategic issues are almost resolved. The influence database (that is, the external and internal factors) becomes the catalyst for generating new strategic issues through itself being updated. However, in the new strategic plan any leftover strategic issues are incorporated (unless it is agreed they should be discarded).

Exhibit 6-17 Selection of a Computer System

Assumptions
A. Enough data analyses and word processing will exist to warrant using a computer.
B. The applications requiring a computer will have a unique mix of numerical analyses, file manipulation, telecommunications word processing and output requirements.
C. Obtaining a computer depends on the tradeoffs among price, service contract, and match to the current and projected uses.

Consideration
A. Decisions whether to buy, lease or lease with option to buy.
B. Examine options of obtaining a computer system for today's needs and later expanding or obtaining a computer system now which you can "grow into."
C. Assess computer systems first on fit between software features and your information processing requirements and second on which hardware can best operate the chosen software.
D. Consider selling unused storage or computer use time to others.
E. Ancillary topics needing to be evaluated include: i) data gathering and entry techniques, ii) special hardware requirements, iii) proper documentation techniques of computer applications, costs, resources usage and problems, iv) maintenance and warranty provisions and v) training.
F. Network with similar computer users to discover solutions to common concerns.

Exhibit 6-18 Reformulation of the Strategic Plan

A. Assess controls and control procedure to ensure obtaining proper results.
B. Make any corrections or alterations to strategic actions, practices or projects to sustain positive outcomes.
C. Define, in advance, the end of the strategic planning cycle. At this time, evaluate and update the influence database.
D. Discover new strategic issues using the influence database.
E. Combine unresolved strategic issues from last "planning cycle" with new strategic issues.
F. Verify through consensus and analysis that strategic issue set is indeed the appropriate one for the firm to deal with at this stage of its evolution. Make any modifications as necessary.
G. Formulate and execute new strategic plan.

From the discovery of new strategic issues does the strategic planning cycle begin anew with one difference over the last cycle: the ability to handle the firm's issues is stronger.

R. Competitive Strengths and Weaknesses.

S. External Opportunities and Threats. R. & S. are discussed for the specific firm example given below.

T. Defining Control Measures. A procedure for defining and using controls during the implementation stage is tantamount to describing the success of the strategic plan. Without controls, implementation can become a chaotic, unplanned and misdirected activity. Exhibit 6-19 presents some common tools (based on Exhibit 5-21) that can easily

Exhibit 6-19 Defining and Applying Control Measures

I. Coming Up with Control Standards
A. Sources
1. Past experience—individuals or firms
2. Professional association
3. Government agency (like National Bureau of Standards)
4. Technical handbooks
5. Experts
B. Verifying Standard
1. Request third-party opinion
2. Circulate proposed standard(s) for feedback
3. Incorporate comments in standard
C. Validating Standard
1. Apply control to several situations
2. Assess results
3. Ascertain validity of standard
4. Concerns may lead to modify standard
5. Verify and validate standard until satisfied with results of control

II. Quality Assurance Plan
A. Definition: use of quality control at several crucial places in the production and dissemination of products or services
B. Application: when
1. Have multiple uses of quality control
2. Do inspection and testing and quality control
3. Carry out quality control during many phases of production or provision
C. Expertise
1. Achieve consensus on quality assurance activities
2. Designate quality assurance inspector and interface duties with consumers
3. Review and update quality assurance plan

Exhibit 6-20 Control Measures in the Beginning Operations Stage

1. Unit cost of:
   A. each input
   B. each output
2. Productivity
3. Demand
4. Profit margin
5. Fit between people and jobs

be applied to carving out an orderly, but specific, method of implementation for the stage at hand. This "method" can be applied to any management, finance, and marketing (the particular controls used for the beginning operations stage) in Exhibit 6-24. Again, the base price for a dance class is less than what the competition charges.

Moving down Exhibit 6-22, the next strategic issue addressed is the one central to this stage: penetrating the student marketplace to generate enough interest to make the classes go. The effort is budget-limited but nonetheless multi pronged: every direct means of informing the students shall be tried. Discussions with teachers, student heads of clubs, the PTA groups, and teachers or officials at recreation centers, clubs, and churches will be done. In addition, displays of posters, leaflets, signs and buttons will be done in the above-mentioned places plus at special community events. Also, word of mouth is carried out at all reasonable times and places as well as with former students of the instructors.

Fourth, broader community publicity is pursued through the yellow pages, local newspapers and a human interest article in the local press. Fifth, requesting local business to carry the school's advertisement is carried out, with class discounts provided to youth affiliated with the business. Together, these channels of reaching and stimulating student interest are geared for short-term response.

The other major facet considered and done here is finding the right people to join the firm. The "right" people means these folks who are competent in dance instruction or office management and equally are willing and wanting to actively contribute to the success of the organization in decision making, communication and leadership (as described in Exhibits 6-10 through 6-12). The strong point for the founder to use is to spend whatever time it takes to feel assured that the new members and she will fully work together as a team.

Thus, the strategic plan for the beginning operation state is shown in Exhibit 6-21. As with the comparable plan in Exhibit 5-22, the elements are

Exhibit 6-21 Strategic Plan for the Beginning Operations Stage

I.   **Firm Definition**

II. **Influence Database**

III. **Strategic Issues and Alternatives**
   A. Daily Operations
   B. Additional Capital
   C. Consumer Description
   D. Output Price
   E. Consumer Market Penetration
   F. Advertising and Promotion Methods
   G. Purchasing
   H. Hiring and Acclimation Methods
   I. Decision Making
   J. Communication Modes
   K. Leadership Guidelines
   L. Cost Reduction
   M. Growth Definition
   N. Information and Control Systems
   O. Contingency Planning
   P. Computer System Selection
   Q. Strategic Plan Reformulation
   R. Competitive Strengths and Weaknesses
   S. External Threats and Opportunities
   T. Defining Control Measures
   U. Control Measures for this Stage

IV. **Decision Criteria**

V.   **Selection of Alternatives**

VI. **Implementation of Alternatives**
   A. Time Table
   B. Summary of positive and negative attributes

VII. **Monitoring**
   A. Feedback
   B. Control Methods

Exhibit 6-22 Strategic Issues and Alternatives for the Beginning Operations Stage of Coplan's School of Dance

Issue	Strategic Alternative(s)	Reasons	Comments
Daily Operations	Able to provide regular and special classes	• Attract high degree of consumer acceptance • Can be tried on limited basis	See Exhibit 6-22
Additional Capital	Have contingent sources and amounts available if needed	• To be adaptive quickly in case of sudden cash need • Large negative impact if need money and have no sources on-line	Prefer debt capital
Consumer Description	Community youth, ages 5-18 currently enrolled in school	• Past and present dance school competitors appeal to this customer group	Later to offer classes to handicapped youth
Output Price	One time charge for a multi week class plus annual registration fee	• Easy to implement • Less cost than competitors • Easily modified for special circumstances of students	See Exhibit 6-23
Consumer Market Penetration	• Past instructed students • Promotion to schools, churches, recreation centers, clubs and families • Advertising in yellow pages, local newspaper, libraries and community businesses • Human-interest article in local newspaper • Listing in community arts directory • Promotion at special community events	• To stimulate long-term interest in taking classes • Implement on limited basis first to see which means produce largest response • Stimulate positive image of firm	Provide class discount to businesses who will display posters

(continued)

Exhibit 6-22 (Continued)

Issue	Strategic Alternative(s)	Reasons	Comments
Advertising and Promotion Methods	• Announcements displayed • Brochures mailed • Arts directory and yellow pages listing • Newspaper story • Special promotions to selected student groups • Media interviews	• Require multimedia effort to penetrate market and stimulate student interest • Combined efforts will increase community recognition	Have business opening celebration
Purchasing	• Cash over credit • Barter acceptable • Purchase in bulk discount whenever possible • Buy direct • Filter and select suppliers	• Quick and cheap to implement • Consistent with firm policies • Keep buying costs low now and in future	
Hiring and Acclimation Methods	• Instructors must be certified by Dance Education of America or completing certification • Instructors must have lived in D.C. area for at least two years • References are checked • Orientation consists of brainstorming concerning working together and service provision • New members are on "parole" for ninety days • Encourage individual work styles and contributions to bettering business	• Consistent with firm definition • Direct connection with development of firm reputation • Effect on competency and continuity of providing dance classes • Impact is long-lasting due to benefits, profit-sharing and working environment	Noninstructor staff have discounts

Issue	Strategic Alternative(s)	Reasons	Comments
Decision Making	• Refrain from making hasty, incomplete decisions • Brainstorm alternatives • Test chosen pathways before full implementation where possible • Obtain sufficient feedback for some decisions	• Reduce conflicts and higher costs • Stimulate team efforts • Allow for individual working styles • Share leadership and response to change • Learn from past mistakes	
Communication Modes	Learn variety of ways to communicate	• Build long-term working relationships • Improve instruction capability • More easily handle resistance or conflict • Costs nothing to implement yet could save a lot of waste	
Leadership Guidelines	All firm members are encouraged to cooperatively exercise and learn	• Affect on team-building • Effect carrying out strategic planning • Direction of firm lies with all participants • Consistent with firm definition • Provide another incentive to stay and grow as firm does	
Cost Reduction	• Any cost incurred comes out of least expensive way to do activity • Periodic assessment of costs to discover how they can be reduced • Incentives provided to incur both inexpensive and wise costs	• Effect sustained cash flow • Effective cost accounting can pave the way for expanded operations • Ensure all members able to reduce costs • Free resources for other uses	

(*continued*)

Exhibit 6-22 (Continued)

Issue	Strategic Alternative(s)	Reasons	Comments
Growth Definition	• Immediate growth in number of students enrolled • Subsequent increase in number of instructors • Next, purchase of new equipment • Outreach to handicapped and community activities • Form dance group • Expand locations	• Increase interest and involvement of community • More resources to breed dance talent • Consistent with firm definition plus modifications • Use additional profits to increase quality of instruction • Achieve reputation in other communities	
Information and Control System	Decide on which data need regularly and consistently collect, what will do with and ways to refine data-gathering efforts	• Affect on firm survival • Affect on sustaining competitive edge • Reduce problems due to faulty data • Vital to doing strategic planning well	
Contingency Planning	• Insurance for fire, flood or vandalism • Founder "will" describe what to do with business if owner becomes unable to run it • Making of scenarios concerning responses to unexpected changes in demand, instructors' abilities, competitors' reactions to firm, etc.	• More effectively carry out strategic planning • Assess steps to turn minor crises into opportunity not catastrophe • Increase degree of adaptive response to external or internal changes	

Issue	Strategic Alternative(s)	Reasons	Comments
Computer System Selection	• Buy a computer system with software appropriate to current needs and ability to expand software and hardware capability as needed • Choose most cost-effective system available	• Required to do everyday paperwork and numerical tasks as well as upgrade information system and influence database • Ensure all members learn how to use it to reduce time spent on standard activities	
Competitive Strengths and Weaknesses	• Flexible and low-price dance instruction • Multifold effort to interest community youth in this school • Qualified instructors • Participatory work environment • Emphasis on holding down costs • Have growth perspective and controls - Effective scheduling of classes - Publicizing of class schedule - Lack of standardized record-keeping procedures - Now fully carrying out orientation of new staff	• Early indication of internal problem areas • Direct effects on provision of dance instruction • Show areas for improvement • Understand trade-off between growth and cost control	

(continued)

Exhibit 6-22 (Continued)

Issue	Strategic Alternative(s)	Reasons	Comments
External Threats and Opportunities	• One competitor recently went out of business • Identify handicapped and senior citizens as two groups who school could appeal to - New disco dancing place to open three miles away - Possible closing of two neighborhood schools in four months	• Test periodic data received from magazines • Give credence to setting up dance school database	
Control Measures	Formulate means of assessing quality of dance instruction provided	• Improve quality of service • Achieve firm objectives • Smarter use of firm resources • Provide additional levels of motivation for firm members	

identical. But the stage builds on the last to further the firm's activities and definition as exemplified at length in Exhibit 5-23.

STRATEGIC PLAN IN ACTION

Based on the last chapter, the final elements are discovered, thought through and incorporated into a strategic plan which will govern the opening and first months of operation for Coplan's School of Dance. Following the format given for a strategic plan, the following observations are seen:

• First, the definition of the firm remains unchanged from the last stage. Clarification of the mission and stribing of this stage.
• Second, the influence database continued to grow as new information is obtained and discovered to support the description of strategic issues and alternatives. The format seen in Exhibit 5-26 is used here as well.

Exhibit 6-23 Daily Operations at Coplan's School of Dance

I. **Service Provisions.** Four kinds of dance classes will be offered, including:
   A. Classical Ballet. A moderate-paced class that's both light and energetic. The student will build strength, balance, grace, and a working movement vocabulary essential for further study.
   B. Modern Jazz. A moderate to fast-paced class that emphasizes a "feeling" and employment of jazz dance rhythms and basic jazz vocabulary. Classes will use a variety of jazz music styles.
   C. Tap. A nonstop movement class with a quick pace. It is designed to develop strength, coordination and endurance from a dance perspective.
   D. Dance Dynamics. A moderately paced class drawing its basic movement vocabulary from a variety of dance disciplines.

II. **Level of Class Difficulty**
   A. Beginning
   B. Intermediate
   C. Advanced

III. **Provision Time**
   A. Each class is one hour
   B. Have classes 4–9 p.m., Monday through Friday and 10 a.m.–5 p.m. on Saturday
   C. Have 43 hours of class per week, with breakdown as follows:
      1. Beginning classes—20 hours
      2. Intermediate classes—13 hours
      3. Advanced classes—10 hours

IV. **Special Classes**
   A. Saturday workshops
   B. Entry in dance festivals
   C. Weekday class beyond standard offerings

V. **Comparison with Competitors**
   A. More class hours per week
   B. Equal number of class varieties
   C. Greater flexibility with special classes

So, using Exhibit 5-6(A), the strategic issues and alternatives for this time period of the firm's evolution are displayed in Exhibit 6-22.

The nexus of firm energy, the daily operations, are detailed in Exhibit 6-23. The orientation is to provide classes in greater numbers, at higher quality and with more flexibility than the competing dance schools in the area. Elizabeth Coplan has several associates who have said that in a pinch they would contribute amounts totaling $15,000 to the school's financial viability. A lot of effort will be channeled to attracting a broad and numerous cross-section of elementary, junior high and high school youth to participate in dance classes. To provide additional incentives to attract students, a pricing scheme is devised and a plan is shown as to how the team can strengthen ties and work through difficulties to remain strong, satisfied and be able to accept new members.

There are "process" facets which the firm members need to consider at this stage, also. These facets include the following:

- developing a means to spend money through evaluating various ways to do so beforehand. The result is both reasonable and effective expenditures.
- putting together a plan for growth. It is never too early to begin thinking about the next steps to firm evolution given that the past ones have been successful. Exhibit 6-22 shows the thoughts the members have about what will come next.
- addressing the "what if" questions which could affect the firm through carrying out contingency planning. The firm members can get together and brainstorm various contingency acts and come up with actions to address them. Then, they can turn the acts and actions into a booklet as an addendum to the strategic plan.
- determining what the ongoing information requirements will be and how best to gather and process such information. This step expands the influence database, coupling it with a specified computer capability. In addition, the data requirements are more clearly delineated between that which is used to support an activity (like accounting or ordering supplies) and that which is used to lead an activity (like new services, additional marketing techniques or better ways of handling problems).

Together, the behavioral and process factors are consciously planned and dealt with in a time frame represented by Exhibit 6-25. What lends the final credibility to implementing the chosen strategic alternatives is control. Exhibit 6-26 demonstrates how controls can be used to assess the operations, results and satisfactions of the School of Dance. The results of control plus the chosen plausible responses to contingencies (Exhibit 6-27) give the information to assess the positive and negative attributes of the firm at this evolutionary stage.

Sample Task 8

What are the positive and negative attributes of Coplan's School of Dance at this point? Do you think the firm is on its way to success? Why?

Further, the outcome of this stage will be the fulfillment of the objective for this stage (given at the end of the last chapter). So, continuing this

Exhibit 6-24 Pricing the Dance Classes

I. **Basic Charges**
   A. Instruction time—$5 per hour
   B. Annual registration—$10 (one-time charge)

II. **Regular Price Scheme**
   A. Weekday Courses
      1. Three times per week, 6 weeks per class
      2. Average cost—$90
   B. Saturday Courses
      1. Two hours per day, 8 weeks per class
      2. Average cost—$80

III. **Special Schemes**
   A. Reduction of each class cost by 10% for students enrolled in two or more classes.
   B. For families with three or more children enrolled, the third and subsequent children pay half price per class.
   C. If a student misses a class period due to illness or emergency, a make-up class may be taken up to three classes per course.
   D. Students may attend a demonstration class free.
   E. Students can earn bonus points based on class performance so that after four classes, a class can be taken for free.
   F. Students who are interested and talented but cannot afford full price are subject to partial scholarship.
   G. If five or more students from the same school "homeroom" sign up for dance classes, each one will receive a coupon good for 20% off the price of the next dance class.

---

sequence, the objectives to be strived for in the next stage of the evolution of Coplan's School of Dance are:

1. To actively have all members use problem-solving procedures within the next six months
2. To have sales of dance products account for 15% of all revenue within the next year
3. To increase consumer population by 25% within the next calendar year
4. To obtain agreement and realization of the most competitive incentive/advancement package for firm members in the next year and a half
5. To develop workable means of responding to change and implement it by all members in the next year

Exhibit 6-25 Time Table to Show Initial Success

Time Frame

Activity	Month 1	Month 2	Month 3	Month 4	Month 5	Month 6	Month 7	Month 8	Month 9	Month 10	Month 11	Month 12
Completely Specify Operations		—										
Schedule Classes											—	
Continue Marketing Efforts		—			—		—		—			
Provide Dance Instructions		—			—		—		—		—	
Develop "Teaming" Perspective					—					—		
Discover Ways of Reducing Costs							—			—		
Initiate Controls									—			
Brainstorm Contingencies								—		—		
Upgrade Information Gathering and Use									—			
Evaluate Controls to Monitor Growth								—		—		—
Modify Strategic Plan as Needed								—		—	—	—

Exhibit 6-26 Using Controls in the Beginning Operations Stage

Control	Measure	Standard	Data Input	Interpretation
Demand	Number of students served per week	160	Registration records	At least 160 separate individuals must be signed up for classes
	Increase in student enrollment	5	Marketing and registration data	If five or more new students are, on average, signing up each week the firm's growth is on target
Instruction Hours	Hours per instructor per week	15–25	Past experience and instruction records	If any instructor teaches less than 15 hours per week, the firm is not profitable. If an instructor teaches more than 25 hours per week, the student performance decreases
Marketing	Individuals contacted per week	40	Contact logs	Numbers are minimum required to obtain increase in student enrollment
	Postings per week	10	Posting records	Information gotten from past experience
	Events attended per week	1	Event notation	
	Businesses responding per week	2	Contact logs	
Profit Margin	*Revenue-Costs* Revenue × 100%	10	Operating records	At least 10% profit needs to be made for the firm to grow

Exhibit 6-27 Response to S.W.O.T.[1]

S.W.O.T.	Point of Discovery	Possible Responses	Comments
Scheduling Adjustments	Response to initial class times	• Offer more classes at certain hours • Increase Saturday classes • Hire another part-time instructor	
Increase in Business Outputs	Approached by entrepreneur developing new dance shoes. Wants to sell exclusively for this area in Dance School	• Expand services to include products • Reject overture • Accept shoes on consignment only • Purchase equity interest in new business through sales of shoes in school	
Loss of School Brochures	Volunteer's home destroyed by fire	• Print up new brochures • Wait and redesign later; canvass by phone • Effort to be interviewed by the media	
Opening of Disco Dance Place	Discovered it as drove by	• Mutual publicity • Offer disco dancing eventually • Ensure dance lesson rates are lower	

[1]Competitive strengths and weaknesses and external opportunities and threats.

Also, the techniques and results of this and the prior stage will carry over and be used in the next stage as required.

Finally, the strategic issues which are carried forth to the next stage are a below-standard profit margin and increasing the outputs to include both dance services and dance products (obtained from Exhibits 6-26 and 6-27). The new strategic plan will be directed toward improving and expanding the basic firm activities to fully gain success with the consumers as well as success with the members.

Chapter 7

Achieving Initial Success

SNAPSHOT

All of the firm's resources are in place. The action has begun, consumers are buying what is offered, operations are occurring, members are learning to interact and contribute, accounting, marketing, and controlling activities are underway and growth is happening. The firm is on its way to becoming noticed, competitive and successful. This stage depicts and demonstrates how initial success is obtained and sustained and what strategic issues need to be encountered and dealt with to ensure the firm's viability. This stage, more than any other, is where "everything seems to work." Yet, as will be shown, it also contains the seeds of future strength or disappearance. As with the previous two chapters, the format of presenting the issues and concepts, then following them with the strategic planning example, will be done.

STRATEGIC ISSUES FOR THE INITIAL SUCCESS STAGE

At this time, the entrepreneur and supporters are concerned about growth—its form and impact—in addition to strategic issues from prior stages (see Exhibit 7-1). These latter issues are, in many cases, reviewed and revised as needed to assist the success profile which is emerging.

Also, by this point in the firm's evolution, an organizational culture and reputation are forming, and they are defined and examined. Third, further emphasis is placed on specifying ways of sustaining member motivation through incentives, member evaluation and career advancement pathways.

Exhibit 7-1 Strategic Issues for Initial Success

- What improvements are needed to the influence database?
- Does the tax structure need to be changed?
- How can problems be solved better?
- What strategic growth pathway is best suited for this stage?
- Which products and/or services are to be provided?
- Which channels have you chosen to reach consumers?
- What pricing scheme will be used?
- What additional sources of financing are required?
- Are any changes to be made to location?
- What organizational structure works and will be improved?
- What are the elements of your organizational culture?
- How can a member evaluation be effectively done?
- What career advancement pathways are viable?
- What incentives are available to firm members, and how should they be provided?
- How should advice or support services be sought?
- Which functional areas will have strategic activities?
- How can the firm establish a sound reputation?
- How can the firm cope effectively with change?
- How will the strategic plan be reviewed?
- What are the firm's competitive strengths and weaknesses at this stage?
- What are the firm's external opportunities and threats at this stage?
- Which control measures are important for this stage?

Finally, a sense of how to deal with change is shown since its influence grows as the firm matures.

A. Influence Database Refinement. The external and internal data collected are the source of identifying strategic issues. Further, the identified strategic issues of Exhibit 7-1 are ranked, implications are determined, and they are separated into immediate and longer-term concerns (see Exhibit 7-2). A proven technique for identifying the primary and secondary effects of strategic issues is called the "Implications Wheel." First developed by Joel Barker, it is used by key players in strategic planning who take the identified issues and brainstorm the plausible impacts these are likely to have on the company, competitors, consumers, society and members. Each player, in turn, describes impacts for the first level. Then, the players again describe secondary impacts and so forth. Next, the issues are prioritized according to the time frame, and impact and strategic alternatives are developed to handle each issue.

Exhibit 7-2 Refining the "Influence" Database

A. Review information obtained from database for accuracy and usefulness.
B. Add or delete data items and sources to obtain more pertinent information.
C. Periodically, prioritize strategic issues for your firm.
D. Use influence database to confirm importance and discover implications for strategic issues.
E. For all strategic issues of interests, look at primary, secondary, and tertiary consequences using the "Implications Wheel."
F. Based on E., specify a set of alternatives to deal with strategic issues of immediate concern.
G. Choose and implement alternatives using decision criteria.
H. Follow strategic issues of longer-range concern to observe an emerging trend. Assess the impact of the trend on the firm.

Sample Task 1

Develop an "Implications Wheel" for the strategic issues of this stage. Discover the implications for the particular concerns affecting your firm. What insights did you learn? Did this technique help, hinder or have no effect on your game plan for progressing your business? Why?

B. Review of the Tax Structure. During this stage, the kind of tax structure the firm has is reexamined to discover whether the size of the firm is compatible with the tax structure, other tax options can give more advantages to the firm, or recent tax developments favor tax structure changes. Working with your accountant and lawyer, the modifications which can be advantageous are determined and are implemented sooner rather than later to reap full benefits.

C. Problem-Solving Procedures. Any firm that is "doing it right" is using effective procedures to handle concerns blocking full achievement or success. As seen in Exhibit 7-3, problems are not only the job of the firm founder but of all firm members who identify and reach solutions as required. The procedure shown here incorporates the decision-making capability of Exhibits 6-10 and 5-6. Also, solving various concerns doesn't only mean dealing with negative situations. The procedures mentioned herein are also equally effective for handling opportunities and strengthening health attributes.

Sample Task 2

Demonstrate how you can use Exhibit 7-3 to prevent problems. Are you ready to take this tack rather than trying only to resolve problems?

Exhibit 7-3 Problem-Solving Procedures

- Sensing—awareness that something is remiss.
- Incubation—indicators keep accumulating out of diverse data. Problem grows and becomes more viable.
- Triggering—point at which problem indicators reach threshold so that the problem is fully recognized.
- Exploration—gather information about causes, symptoms and current effects.
- Definition—state essence of the problem.
- Consensus—gain feedback and viewpoint to confirm the problem statement.
- Search—delineate alternative means of resolving the problem.
- Generate decision criteria—specify "filters" for choice.
- Choose—state those alternatives needed to resolve the problem.
- Implement—put the solution(s) into effect.
- Control—monitor and modify "answers" as required.

D. Strategic Growth Pathway. During this stage, the firm needs to determine what means it will use to grow in a strong way. Using Exhibit 6-14 as a base, the firm specifies the rate, timing, emphases and controls of growth. That is, given that sales, income, profit, member satisfaction, item quality, market share, reputation, consumer acceptance, etc., are all rising, how does the firm effectively sustain and monitor the balance among these factors while output increases? The firm example described below will demonstrate how this company deals with it.

Sample Task 3

Specify three rates of growth, say, slow, moderate and fast. Which "rate" will you pursue at this stage? Why? What supporting tools will you need to achieve the growth rate selected?

E. Product/Service Choice. By this point the firm has clear ideas of which items it will present to the marketplace. This stage gives further time to refine such items to make them even more attractive to the present or projected clients or customers (see Exhibit 7-4 for the method).

F. Client/Customer Channels. As with E, these are also defined to give more straightforward ways of reaching intended consumers. Based on earlier experience and the suggestions of Exhibit 7-5, the demand is creatively yet carefully stimulated for the firm's items. Again, growth is not best if it is greatest and fastest. Growth works if it is measured against what the firm can reasonably absorb and handle.

Exhibit 7-4 Choice of Products and/or Services

- Redefine specific goods or services you provide currently.
- Discuss which items have done well, which ones have done okay, and which ones have done poorly. State reasons why.
- Describe alterations to items which have done well to make them more attractive.
- Give rationale for keeping or disposing of existing items which are not "best seller."
- Specify volume level(s) of items you wish to obtain with justification.
- Summarize products and/or services to provide knowledge of their inter-relationships.

Exhibit 7-5 Client/Customer Channels

1. Who are your buyers? Give complete, detailed description.
2. What do they buy, when, and in what manner?
3. How have your buyers changed since you began offering your items to them? Why have the changes occurred?
4. How do new buyers learn of your items?
5. What are your best means of stimulating demand? Worst means? Okay means?
6. Discuss how to improve demand stimulation procedures. Will you delete means which have not done well?
7. Summarize actions to sustain and later increase consumer demand for your items.

G. Pricing Scheme Refinement. Apart from returning larger profit per unit sale, the pricing scheme alterations allow for longer-term profit planning; that is, to become and remain competitive not only for a season, item life cycle or calendar year, but for as long as the firm wishes. To do so requires coming up with a set of options which together can give the needed direction for sustained demand. Exhibit 7-6 demonstrates how to arrive at such options.

H. Additional Sources of Financing. Specification of consumer items and market channels occur in each stage. As well, so does discovering if more capital is required. The decision template presented in Exhibit 6-3 can also be used here for making such a determination. The key is to obtain enough money to finance the growth pathway—too much can be as deleterious as too little.

I. Change in Location? In a sense, this factor is self-evident. If the firm has expanded beyond its current facilities, larger ones must be found. On the other hand, location is also a function of the service or product you are providing. The less critical the factor, the more choice and flexibility the firm has over the kind and location of "quarters." Exhibit 7-7

Exhibit 7-6 Refining the Pricing Scheme

A. What has worked about the way items are priced?
B. What has not worked in pricing the items?
C. What alternatives are available for pricing? By:
   1. Volume
   2. Season
   3. Consumer
   4. Location
   5. Competitors
   6. Gimmick (constant sale, free item. Free delivery, etc.)
   7. Day-of-the-week
   8. Special Event
   9. Barter
D. Which options for price coordination?
   1. Number of different pricing schemes required
   2. Number of different items per pricing scheme
E. Choices for pricing elements and scheme(s)
F. Pricing scheme decision with rationale

Exhibit 7-7 Is It Time to Change Location?

I.   Past Experience
   A. Advantages of present location
   B. Disadvantages of present location
   C. Usefulness of present location

II. Current Requirements
   A. Reasons to stay put
   B. Reasons to change or expand location (customers, members, markets and resources)
   C. Options for location (buy, lease, lease with option to buy; other financial incentives)

III. Location Actions
   A. Priority for options
   B. Decision criteria (cost, transportation commute, conveniences, service, security, space readiness, environmental amenities, labor pool, cost of living, offices layout, internal environment, etc.)
   C. Choice of location directions

IV. Monitoring and Evaluation of Implemented Actions

gives some pointers to use when considering a move. However, efficient use of space is more important than luxury of space.

J. Organizational Structure. Based on the earlier discussion of Exhibit 5-20, the firm now decides which guiding principles and practices are appropriate and effective to achieve the firm's definition. Exhibit 7-8 reviews the elements and has the members make suggestions for "structure." Then through consensus, the firm decides on the form to use for future growth. Such a choice is based on the firm particulars, not on any preset molds into which the firm must fit. Yet, more and more, structure is being defined based on information needs. This implies that: i) hierarchies are being replaced by networks, and ii) authority and decision making are becoming more decentralized.

Exhibit 7-8 Overall Structure for the Organization

I. **Describe the specific elements for the firm today:**
   A. Division of labor
   B. Communication modes
   C. Distribution of authority
   D. Functions of message flow
   E. Responsibility
   F. Incentives
   G. Corporate culture
   H. Coordination
   I. Motivation
   J. Resistance to change
   K. Work climate
   L. Span of control
   M. Departmentalization
   N. Structure
   O. Control

II. **Write a one-paragraph description of the best and worst characteristics of the organization.** Explain how to improve or change the worst aspects and how to better the best aspects.

III. **Obtain feedback on which organizational choice is highly desired for the structure.**

IV. **List and rank the structure choices.**

V. **Use decision criteria and choose the structural form.**

VI. **Implement new or sustain "existing" structure.**

VII. **Monitor and upgrade structure as needed.**

Sample Task 4

Come up with a scheme for operating an organization with no job titles, descriptions, hierarchy, autocratic rules or main authority. Could your organization work well? Why? Would you be willing to consider a shared management motif for the "structure"?

K. Organizational Culture. Enough interaction and layers are associated with the firm to naturally evolve a culture. Exhibit 7-9 succinctly describes what constitutes a culture and what applications the culture has to making the firm a better place to contribute, to accomplish and to handle change. Such a culture is unique to each firm. If used (rather than abused), it can be an invaluable asset to long-term viability, since all "behavioral" aspects of the firm can be enhanced by the culture.

Sample Task 5

Define precisely what elements will make up your organizational culture. Why do you need them, and how will you use them?

L. Member Evaluation. Members are concerned that their performance will not be properly monitored. One of the best ways to correct this concern and provide the basis for further motivation is the member evaluation.

The salient factors are depicted in Exhibit 7-10. Together, these give a blueprint for developing a performance assessment which can be augmented or tailored to suit individual, group or full firm membership requirements.

Exhibit 7-9 Defining an Organizational Culture

I.   Elements
  A. Norms: guidelines and insights about individual and group behavior
  B. Rituals: activities, traditions and stories done to reinforce and further ways of thinking and/or acting
  C. Symbols: concise representations of the firm to members, consumers, suppliers, competitors, regulators, and other groups

II. Applications
  A. Define and further motivate mean and performance levels of firm individuals
  B. Understand, achieve and sustain cooperation among firm members
  C. Accomplish all aspects of firm definition
  D. Handle external changes and/or internal innovations

Exhibit 7-10 Conducting a Member Evaluation

A. Time Frame
   1. Periodically
   2. As needed
B. Location
   1. On site
   2. Off site
C. Evaluators
   1. Individual
   2. Group
D. Process
   1. Standardized
   2. Tailored to member
E. Evaluation Features
   1. Fast or slow time period
   2. Simple or complex procedure
   3. Objective or subjective emphasis
   4. Detailed or general elements examined
F. Elements for an Evaluation
   1. Strengths
   2. Weaknesses
   3. Performance to date
   4. Career potential
   5. Suggested actions
   6. Comments
   7. Member's feedback
G. Impact of Evaluations with Reasons
   1. Little change
   2. Moderate change
   3. Large change
H. Means to Improve Evaluation
   1. More participation
   2. Less formality
   3. Indicators which measure performance
   4. Greater use of results
   5. Two-way feedback

Sample Task 6

Devise a method of evaluating the evaluators. Do you think the feedback gained is worth the time and effort to obtain it? Why?

M. Career Advancement Pathways. Performance evaluations are important tools for periodic assessments of member activities. Yet, a sequence of such evaluations does not create a career pathway. Instead, Exhibit 7-11 presents the variables necessary to formulate a means

Exhibit 7-11 Career Advancement Pathways

A. Theme
  1. Up or out
  2. Continuous achievement
  3. Seniority
B. Judgment Means
  1. Member evaluation
      a. Self
      b. Peer
      c. Group
      d. Other
  2. Relationship to founder(s)
  3. Income level relative to:
      a. Other income levels
      b. Achievements of others at same income level
      c. Other firms
  4. Impacts of accomplishments on:
      a. Firm members
      b. Business operations
      c. Growth potential
      d. Society
      e. Other
C. Time Frame
  1. Short term only
  2. Short-intermediate term
  3. Intermediate-long term
  4. Long term only
D. Member feedback
  1. Career aspirations and professional growth
  2. Career relationship to education
  3. Career relationship to family
  4. Fulfill certain standards
  5. "Funnel" selection
E. Compatibility between member feedback and advancement theme

of longer-term personal and professional advancement. The company example shown below will identify examples of such pathways.

N. Firm Member Incentives. For either performance assessment or career advancement, an important motivating factor is incentives. Exhibit 7-12 shows some incentives. To ascertain the mix of incentives desired and meaningful to firm members, group consensus is required. The mix of incentives is likely to expand and change as the firm matures.

O. Advice and Support Services. Another "housekeeping" task which occurs here is to rethink whether the advice and support the firm is getting from current experts is valid and continued useful. If not, then finding new sources of say, legal or accounting support is done. Further, other sources of advice may be needed during this stage, including:

- marketing
- advertising
- promotion
- production
- personnel
- strategic planning
- investments
- growth options
- office, computer or facilities management
- other

As Exhibit 7-13 demonstrates, whenever possible, choose advice from among firm members; only if conditions or lack of talent dictate should outside experts be consulted.

Exhibit 7-12 Incentives for Firm Members

"Basic"
- Salary
- Health, life disability and other insurance
- Sick and holiday leave
- Vacation time
- Education reimbursement
- Retirement plan
- Bonus
- Fitness program

"Advanced"
- Employee stock ownership
- Profit-sharing
- Company items and facilities
- Company discounts and special events
- Intrapreneurship

Exhibit 7-13 Seeking Advice and Support Services

I.   **Factors**
     A. Inside/outside the firm
     B. Formal or informal
     C. One time or ongoing
     D. New or revised
     E. Reasons
        1. Crisis
        2. Serious problems
        3. Fine-tuning of existing concerns
        4. New ideas or methods
        5. Unavailability of required resources or know-how
        6. Following example of other firms

II. **Types of Support**
     A. Single or multiple operational areas
     B. Single or multiple problems
     C. One or more advisors and/or firms

III. **Means of Choosing Providers**
     A. Need for objectivity
     B. Confidentiality
     C. Reputation of providers
     D. Ease of implementing solution
     E. Cost, barter, or benefits to advisors

P. Functional Strategic Activities. At this stage, many firms de facto form various functional areas, setting up a marketing department, personnel department, accounting department, executive suite and, if needed, production department, research and development department, distribution department and so forth. But, separate departments need not be a foregone by-product of firm growth. Instead, based on Exhibit 7-8, the firm members can delineate the priority of functional strategic issues and which members or member groups should handle them. Exhibit 7-14 gives some guidance in this regard.

Q. Establishing a Reputation. As the firm's activities grow, so do its impacts. Over time, these impacts take the form of a reputation as feedback and responses from consumers, supplies, industry representatives, competitors, regulators and members occur. Yet, a reputation need not be established "helter-skelter." There are distinct channels which can be used to think ahead about the form and content of the reputation. These channels are mentioned in Exhibit 7-15. The quality and content of the reputation can effect the positive acts of both members and consumers.

Exhibit 7-14 Functional Strategic Activities

Guidelines for each functional area:
- Summary of past activities
- Current situation
- Functional objectives (as related to corporate objectives)
- Functional strategic issues
- Resolution pathways for functional strategic issues
- Controls for implementation and responsibilities
- Application of resolution to other functional areas
- Obtained from strategic plan

Exhibit 7-15 Establishing a Reputation

I. **External Indicators**
  A. Consumer satisfaction
  B. Supplier comments
  C. Media opinion
  D. Competitors' perspective
  E. Industry/trade association representatives' viewpoints

II. **Internal Indicators**
  A. Members opinions and viewpoints
  B. Correlation between firm philosophy and members' attitudes
  C. Members' desires and actions toward firm improvement
  D. Orienting firm culture to heighten reputation

III. **Applications**
  A. Initial strategic plan
  B. Review of influence database
  C. Career advancement and member evaluation control measures
  D. Relations with the public

Sample Task 7

What kind of reputation do you want your firm to have? Once you achieve it, do you want the reputation to be sustained? Can it be?

R. Coping with Change. By the act of getting up in the morning, change is inevitable. The importance of change and its response opportunities remain whether the firm members take advantage of it or not. However, if the members believe in other than the ostrich approach, Exhibit 7-16 discusses what change is and how to effectively exploit it. Sensitive leadership can first discover those change issues which offer a high

Exhibit 7-16 Coping with Change

I.   Definition—ability to adjust, modify or adapt to different conditions
II. Process
    A. Acknowledge present situation
    B. Identify factors which are varying
    C. Assess impacts of factors on situation
    D. Understand responses required to continue or increase viability of situation
    E. Implement and monitor responses
III. Attitude

A. Positive	B. Negative
1. Fact of life	1. Rejecting
2. Fun	2. Ill-informed
3. Challenging	3. Uncomfortable
4. Open to it	4. Mistrust
5. Gives personal growth	5. See no benefit

IV. Impacts

A. Negative	B. Positive
1. Stress	1. Increased competition
2. Resistance to change	2. Better operated firm
3. Conflict	3. Higher quality communication
4. Alienation	4. Successful use of strategic planning
5. Conforming to group norm	5. More responsive to members' and consumer's needs

V.   Means to overcome negative impacts
    A. Practice in open communication
    B. Acknowledging specific impacts and addressing ways to mitigate them
    C. Greater participation in strategic planning
    D. Incentives to discover potential changes *early*
    E. Emphasis on refining means to handle changes

probability of resolution in a relatively short time frame. Then, move on to tougher issues. Effective use of change can be the basis for a sustained competitive advantage. Again, the company example below will show how change is put into "action" to benefit the firm.

S.   Strategic Plan Review. The process of strategic planning is examined at this point to ascertain whether any improvements or alterations are required. If so, based on Exhibit 2-1, modifications are quickly decided upon and put into place. Exhibit 7-17 poses some monitoring questions to discover what changes may be required. Whatever the outcome, the strategic planning method will continue to be learned and used by all members.

T.   Competitive Strengths and Weaknesses.

Exhibit 7-17 Questioning the Strategic Planning Process

- What information sources (inside or outside the company) should now be tapped?
- Are the strategic issues being given proper emphasis, discovery, evaluation, priority and resolution?
- What decision criteria needs to be added, deleted or changed?
- Are resources available to continue to do effective implementation?
- How much influence has strategic planning had on the company's overall success and achieving the firm's definition?
- What areas of the process need improvement, and how will these improvements occur?
- What kinds of member behavior have constrained strategic planning from being totally successful?
- Which future directions, that are now here, does strategic planning need to follow?
- What ways are available for effectively involving more firm members in strategic planning?
- Has sufficient, accurate and objective feedback been sought out from "devil's advocates" or expert consultants?

U. External Opportunities and Threats. U. and V. are discussed at length in the company examples shown below.

V. Control Measures. At any stage, effective means of evaluating key aspects of the firm and/or operations is an important additional "check" on the firm viability. Based on Exhibit 6-18, some measures applicable to this stage are given in Exhibit 7-18 and applied in the company example below. Thus, the strategic plan for this stage is given as in Exhibit 7-19.

STRATEGIC PLAN IN ACTION

Up until now, strategic planning has been used to set the stage, gather the actors and begin the performance. Yet, the proof of the efforts is how well received are the business activities. This stage of the firm's evolution concentrates on having Coplan's School of Dance become successful.

One of the first actions taken here is to refine the influence database so that the information derived from it can directly be used in keeping records, making decisions, taking actions, doing modifications and pursuing new directions. Using Exhibit 7-20 as the template for identifying and handling strategic issues, the primary emphasis will be to continue and deepen the balance between behavioral and process activities.

The behavioral side emphasizes: bettering problem-solving capabilities, deciding on the kind of organizational structure and culture the members desire,

Exhibit 7-18 Control Measures in Initial Success Stage

1. Match between firm outputs and users
2. Relationship between management capacity and output
3. Return on investment
4. Rate of productivity
5. User satisfaction
6. Demand rate
7. Quality of output
8. Efficiency of information use
9. Influence of founders
10. Effectiveness of:
    a. Problem-solving
    b. Meetings
    c. Feedback
    d. Project management
11. Percent of accounts receivable or payable to total sales
12. Degree of member satisfaction
13. Ability to cope with change

recognizing whether every member has enough avenues to contribute to and receive from the organization, and an understanding of how to further the firm's reputation and deal with change.

The process side emphasizes expanding the variety of outputs (and as a consequence requiring purchasing knowledge), focusing the marketing efforts, altering the pricing scheme, rethinking the need for outside advice, and reviewing the entire planning effort. A time table is prepared (as in Exhibit 7-21) to demonstrate how initial success will occur. Notice that several of the activities are repeated in intervals so as to verify and improve the previous attempts. A sample of the kinds of controls which can be used herein is shown in Exhibit 7-22. Also, responses to important strengths, weaknesses, opportunities or threats the dance school faces during this stage are given in Exhibit 7-23.

Overall, Coplan's School of Dance is in good health and likely to sustain it if close watch on the marketplace and internal workings continue.

Sample Task 8

What are the central, positive accomplishments which must occur for, say, your firm to become successful? What are the central, negative constraints to this objective? Has Coplan's School of Dance achieved initial success? Why?

Exhibit 7-19 Strategic Plan for the Initial Success Stage

I. **Firm Definition**

II. **Influence Database**

III. **Strategic Issues and Alternatives**
   A. Influence Database Refinement
   B. Review Tax Structure
   C. Problem-Solving Procedures
   D. Strategic Growth Pathway
   E. Product/Service Choice
   F. Client/Customer Channels
   G. Pricing Scheme Refinement
   H. Additional Sources of Financing
   I. Change in Location
   J. Organizational Structure
   K. Organizational Culture
   L. Member Evaluation
   M. Career Advancement Pathways
   N. Firm Member Incentives
   O. Advice and Support Services
   P. Functional Strategic Activities
   Q. Establishing a Reputation
   R. Coping with Change
   S. Strategic Plan Review
   T. Competitive Strengths and Weaknesses
   U. External Opportunities and Threats
   V. Control Measures

IV. **Decision Criteria**

V. **Selection of Alternatives**

VI. **Implementation of Alternatives**
   A. Time table
   B. Summary of positive and negative attributes

VII. **Monitoring**
   A. Feedback
   B. Control methods

**Exhibit 7-20 Strategic Issues and Alternatives for the
Initial Success Stage of Coplan's School of Dance**

Issue	Strategic Alternative(s)	Reasons	Comments
Influence Database Refinement	• Give priority to data inputs • Expand sources to reflect current data needs • Develop master list of external and internal data items • Distinguish between data of short-range concern and data of longer-range concern	• Increase viability of information use • Minimize time and cost • Become more able to respond to changing conditions	
Problem Solving	• All members share in training a practice of problem solving • Distinguish, prioritize and more clearly respond to problems	• Improve management capability • Shared acceptance and mutual activity • Reinforce decision making • Positive impacts of long duration	
Outputs Selection	• Expand to include sales of dance outfits and shoes	• Increase revenue • Broaden and stabilize outputs • Can try on limited basis • High potential for consumer acceptance	
Marketing Channels Focus	• Build on referrals • Conduct oral surveys • Make presentation on dance to student groups	• Minimal cost and little time • Improve consumer acceptance • Additional creative avenue for firm members • Draw more dedicated students for multiple classes	

Issue	Strategic Alternative(s)	Reasons	Comments
Pricing Scheme Alteration	• Select those means which make money • Add discounts for joint dance class and clothing purchase • Give rebate to students with high performance • Use barter to accomplish "legwork"	• Attract more students • Increase reputation of firm • Easy member and student acceptance • Implement on limited basis first	See Exhibit 6-23
Changing Location			Facilities adequate for current activities
Organizational Structure	• Members participate in training • Together evaluate how to improve organization	• Strengthen ability with workflow • Reduce resistance to tackling problems and handling changes • Sustain cohesive yet self-directed organization	
Organizational Culture Recognition	• Cooperative, shared leadership and innovation • Informal outings, get-togethers and physical activities • Logo, work outfits, card and brochure with "dance step" ensignia	• Fulfill firm definition • Describe firm to members and outsiders equally • Guide evolution of organization	
Evaluation of Members	• Developed by members for members • Subject to improvement • Evaluation is timely, thorough, fair and leads to strengthening performance	• Provide additional motivation and incentives • Have yet another reason for team work • Fulfill firm definition • Key is member acceptance	

(continued)

Exhibit 7-20 (Continued)

Issue	Strategic Alternative(s)	Reasons	Comments
Career Advancement	• As firm grows so will members' challenge, achievements, influence and innovation • Advance to actualizing abilities not to another position • Each member's advancement tailored to member lifestyle	• Provide incentives to stay through long term • Can be tried on limited basis first • More you give, the more you share in benefits • Provide model of organization development for students to understand	
Incentives	• Determined by and for members • Modified as member groups grow and change	• Impact is less than in other firms • Provide additional motivation • Means of increasing diversity of activities	
Advice and Support	• Continue to use existing lawyer and accountant • Additional advice obtained through informal discussion with colleagues	• Thus far, pleased with advice and counsel of professionals • Cost effective to obtain advice informally	
Establishing a Reputation	• Obtain feedback from students • Distill member perspectives • Solicit parents, teachers and competitors	• Fulfill firm definition • Increase quality and satisfaction of activities • Enlarge respect • Have long-term impact as viable competitor	Use comments to further outreach and service provision efforts
Coping with Change	• Use strategic planning to detect, analyze and respond to changes	• Previous success in doing so • Long-term positive impact • Effective use of people and resources	
Reviewing Strategic Planning	• Evaluate as would a member • Consensually agree on ways to strengthen process	• Lifeblood of firm's survival • Allow for more complete attainment of firm goals • Can sustain and enhance growth efforts	

Issue	Strategic Alternative(s)	Reasons	Comments
Competitive Strengths and Weaknesses	• Strong, together organization • Dance instruction is of high quality • Using strategic planning to the fullest - Marketing producing sporatic results - Turnover of part-time clerical help high - Professionals spend too much time doing bookkeeping - Classrooms are underused	• Prepare for further growth • Assess interactions among all organizational elements • Discover redundancies and waste	
External Opportunities and Threats	• Potential to expand barter with area businesses • Proposal to reduce physical education activity in high schools • Local dance group is relocating • Building owner thinking about selling - Competitors are stepping up marketing efforts - Competitors are reducing prices - Elementary schools' enrollment down by 20% from last year - Utilities costs jumped by 80%	• Early warning system to respond to external events • Need to resolve these issues as prelude to next stage • Sustain competitive capability	Coordinate actions with internal responses
Controls	• Measure all vital signs of firm's activities • Another means of identifying improvement actions	• Monitor strategic planning • Specify what works, what doesn't and what else to do	

Exhibit 7-21 Timetable to Prepare for Expansion

Activity	Month 1	Month 2	Month 3	Month 4	Month 5	Month 6	Month 7	Month 8	Month 9	Month 10 ... Month 18
Refine Influence Database		▬								
Institute Problem-Solving		▬▬▬								
Modify Outputs	▬▬▬▬▬									
Refocus Marketing Channels								▬▬▬		
Alter Pricing Scheme					▬▬▬▬▬▬▬▬					
Refine Organizational Structure and Culture				▬▬▬▬▬▬						
Describe Member Evaluation, Career Advancement and Incentive Paths								▬		
Review Strategic Planning				▬▬▬▬▬▬▬						
Learn about Coping with Change			▬▬▬▬▬▬▬▬							
Upgrade Service Provision			▬▬▬▬▬▬▬							
Handle Competitive Strengths and Weaknesses						▬▬▬▬				
Handle External Opportunities and Threats			▬▬▬▬							▬▬▬
Institute Controls			▬▬▬▬							▬▬▬

Time frame

Exhibit 7-22 Using Controls in the Initial Success Stage

Control	Measure	Standard	Data Input	Interpretation
Output/User Match	Skills change per student	3	Performance evaluation of students	Improvement in three skill areas at end of a class
Output/Member	Students per instructors	80	Registration records	Minimum number of students to turn a profit
Productivity Rate	Change in new students taught per instructor per class	+ 5	Registration records	Minimum number for growth
Student Satisfaction	Indicators per evaluation	Outstanding	Evaluation of courses	Rating of outstanding or better on 80% or more of course indicators
Demand Rate	New students per month	20	Outcome of marketing effort questionnaire	Minimum number of students to sustain growth rate
Output Quality	Comparison per student	Good or better rating	Questionnaire	Requests students to compare quality of learning with competitors' classes
Information Use Efficiency	Time from access to use	3 weeks	Monitoring of information	Minimum time before decision made about information application
	Information used divided by total information obtained	40%	Monitoring of information	Minimum amount to justify time and cost expenditures

(*continued*)

Exhibit 7-22 (Continued)

Control	Measure	Standard	Data Input	Interpretation
Influence of Founders	Number of decisions divided by total decisions	40%	Decision records	Members agree that founder should, at most, make no more than 40% of the major decisions
Effectiveness of Problem Solving	Problems unsolved divided by total problems solved	20%	Monitoring problem solutions	If 20% or more of problems remain unsolved over, say, a three-month interval, improvements are needed
Financial Viability	Accounts receivable to total revenue	30%	Accounting records	If either of these percentages is met or exceeded, the financial health of the firm is threatened
	Accounts payable to total revenue	20%	Accounting records	
Member Growth	Areas of satisfaction divided by total number of work aspects	60%	Member questionnaire	If percentage is less than this amount, members need to consider ways to improve benefits derived
Change Successes	Number of changes positively dealt with divided by total changes	70%	Change records	If less than 70% of all changes are dealt with positively, strategic planning process need be improved

Exhibit 7-23 Response to S.W.O.T.[1]

S.W.O.T.	Point of Discovery	Possible Response	Comments
Ineffective Marketing	Trend based on prior results	• Focus marketing efforts to only a few key actions • Discover how to strengthen actions taken • Ensure actions will not be in conflict	
Part-time Turnover	Trend based on last 18 months	• List reasons for leaving • Discover common threads in turnover • Correct "threads" and initiate improvements to work environment • More carefully screen potential members	
Bookkeeping Time	Observation over last six months	• Have accountant perform more book-keeping tasks • Automate tasks using in-house computer • Hire part-time student to do bookkeeping	
Underused Classrooms	Schedule records	• Rent out space to other groups • Schedule more classes • Institute special programs	
Barter Expansion	Past experience with area businesses	• Increase amount and variety of barter with existing players • Pursue barter with other businesses • Increase barter with students to reduce pressure to hire new staff	

(continued)

Exhibit 7-23 (Continued)

S.W.O.T.	Point of Discovery	Possible Response	Comments
Reduction of Physical Education in High Schools	School board meeting	• Develop tailored brochure for parents • Distribute brochure as mailing or hand out at "parent" events	
Possible Sale of Building	Discussion with building owner	• Relocate • Modify lease so can stay if building changes ownership • Find other tenants and together purchase building • Take action against owner for health code violations	
Marketing from Competition	Informal discussions with students and promotional literature	• Upgrade marketing • Counter competitor marketing with classes, pricing or scheduling to sustain niche	
Competitors' Price Reduction	Discussion with instructors in other schools	• Ensure your prices and pricing schemes are better than competition • Expand discount opportunities	
Decrease in Elementary School	Discussion with elementary school teachers	• Emphasize retaining existing students • Focus on attracting older students	
Utilities Cost Increase	Cost statements from companies	• Pass along costs in registration fee • Decrease hours of operation • Sublease space	

¹Competitive strengths and weaknesses and external opportunities and threats.

As with previous stages, new objectives are developed at this time for use in the next stage. In our case, these objectives would be:

A. To reinvest 20% of profits in the business and invest the other 80% in growth stocks by the end of the next quarter
B. To ensure that every instructor (in the next six months) spends at least five minutes a month with every student individually
C. To generate 15% of adult dance instruction population within the next year
D. To sell $50,000 in own dance wear design in the last half of this year
E. To reduce waste by 50% in next six months; 80% in next nine months; and 90% in next eighteen months
F. To hire and train four new instructors in the next nine months

In addition, the prior and present techniques and results discussed herein compound and are used as needed in the next stages.

Finally, the strategic issues from this stage which will carryover to the next stage are clarifying and strengthening the influence database, the organizational structure and member relations. This statement is based on a poor showing in implementation control of information use efficiency, change successes and member growth. The new strategic plan produced will be oriented to growth without sacrifice of member cohesiveness and consumer relations.

Chapter 8

Expanding the Firm

SNAPSHOT

Your organization has, by this time, come a long way. From idea through firm definition through decision to operate, the business has gathered resources, defined activities, begun operations, instituted controls, obtained marketplace recognition, achieved sales growth, instituted information and incentive programs, solved problems, did contingency planning, articulated growth and change directions and evolved an organizational culture. All of these activities occurred using strategic planning within the influence of the founding members. Now, however, such influence will, of necessity, change. As the firm moves into this chapter's mode—expansion—the following concerns must be met:

- redefine the influence and day-to-day direction of the original members;
- match the pressures for conformity and standardization with those for autonomy and creative issue resolution;
- carefully monitor new operations to improve both them and the existing ones;
- coordinate and integrate firm activities around the original firm definition;
- evaluate success in the short term versus success in the long term;
- improve communication and skills of firm members;
- test contingency plans;
- obtain whatever additional financing is required; and
- grow well.

As Exhibit 8-1 shows, the composite response to the strategic issues listed will make the difference between growing strong or not.

Exhibit 8-1 Discovering Strategic Issues for Expansion

- What additional capital sources are needed to finance expansion?
- Should the firm go public? Why?
- Which investments are appropriate to consider?
- How will consumers be impacted by expansion?
- Which changes, if any, should be made to the organizational structure?
- Should modifications occur to the firm's items or their price scheme?
- What improvements are needed to the growth plan?
- Are revisions needed to the influence database?
- What trade-offs between short and long-term success need be dealt with?
- Which refinements are appropriate for using internal staff or outside advisors?
- Do contingency plans work?
- How can member working relationships be enhanced?
- In what areas will the firm increase involvement with social responsibility?
- How will the firm identify and reduce waste?
- Which means will be chosen to handle resistance to change and conflicts?
- What means will be used to learn from failure?
- What are the firm's external opportunities and threats at this stage?
- What are the firm's internal strengths and weaknesses at this stage?
- What control measures are used by the firm at this stage?

STRATEGIC ISSUES FOR EXPANSION STAGE

A. Additional Capital Amounts. In each stage thus far, concerns with financing have been discussed. This stage is no different except for one crucial point—the quantities of money obtained are for the long term. That is, whether the funds be loans, loan guarantees, public stock offerings, issuance of bonds, venture capital or large equity investors, the money will be used to finance the expansion activities over months and years. This means that the firm must have an effective accounting system in place to closely monitor and deal with any cash flow, interest, or repayment problems which will erode the firm's projects. Immediate sales growth must be counterweighed by later cost growth so as not to endanger the financial viability of the firm. Exhibit 8-2 lists the crucial factors which must be kept in mind in obtaining funds.

B. Public Offering. Financial circumstances are conducive today to issuing stock in the firm for public purchase. More companies are doing so than in the past. Yet, there are trade-offs. Questions to be answered include:

- Can funds be directly secured in other ways at more favorable financing terms?

Exhibit 8-2 Concerns with Using and Finding More Money

I. **Using Funds**
  A. Total amount required
  B. Timeframe of applications
  C. Kinds of expenditures
  D. Impacts on profitability
  E. Impacts on financial solvency
  F. Improvements in finance and accounting systems required

II. **Locating Funds**
  A. Mixture of debt and equity capital
  B. Priority of sources
  C. Timing of funds receipt
  D. Special conditions for funds receipt

- Are firm founders and members willing to give up some internal leadership for public disclosure requirements of an initial public offering?
- Will enough capital be raised in the time allotted?
- If the firm is not a corporation, do the members wish to change the ownership structure?

To make this decision requires figures having a full amount of useful information. Exhibit 8-3 points out the factors which can lead to the complete profile required.

Sample Task 1

Develop a plan for going public as soon as possible. What conditions must be satisfied and actions occur before you can do so?

  C. Firm Investments. Exhibit 8-4 shows what you need to know before making an investment with the firm's projects. Two key elements which should be highly considered along with return are the risk and the profile of the investee. Risk is difficult to quantify but does include such factors as:
  - past experience of the industry;
  - financial solvency of the firm;
  - degree to which business activities done previously;
  - alternative investments with similar return pattern;
  - whether investment funds are "discretionary" or "vital."

Exhibit 8-3 Deciding Whether or Not to Go Public

Considerations/Conditions
- Recent trend among small businesses
- Amount of money needed and its time frame
- Proliferation of investors
- New measures of firm's financial health
- Timing to issue stock publicly
- Value of investment better than venture capital or other equity
- Item(s) provided are in high demand
- Cannot meet capital requirements privately
- Proper selection of professional assistance (underwriter, auditor and lawyer) is a must unless doing it yourself
- Discuss going public with executives of comparable firms who recently went public

Constraints
- Dilute founder's ownership equity and, in some cases, redirect leadership
- Need corporate ownership form before issuing stock
- Having filing and reporting requirements with the Security and Exchange Commission
- Require plan for marketing stock in aftermarket to draw new stockholders
- Amount of capital raised varies depending on stock terms and public response

Advantages
- Initial Public Offering (IPO) can provide stock option as additional incentive to members
- Stock can be used for acquisition actions
- Equity generated from IPO can form basis for future financing
- Publicity and new investors can boost sales

The profile of the investee is important since not only does your firm want to make money, but to see that the investee's use your investment for one or more beneficial purposes to society. Choosing, therefore, which concerns to invest in involves more than just which one will yield the highest amount in the shortest time.

Sample Task 2

Do a trade-off analysis among three options for distributing profit:

1. disseminate it to founders or founder and members;
2. reinvest it in the business;
3. invest it in longer-term, income-producing alternatives.

Which one or combination would you choose? Why?

Exhibit 8-4 Investments by the Firm

Factors
- Financial solvency of company
- Amount desired to invest
- Time frame of investing and investments
- Benefits derived by each investment
- Risks of each investment
- Alternatives to investment
- Investee's characteristics (i.e., history, purpose, activities, success measures, projected actions, ethnics, and other)

Types
- Stocks in private firms, institutional funds or commodities
- Bonds in utility or city organizations
- Money market funds
- Seed capital money for start-ups
- Venture capital to existing companies
- Insurance
- Real estate
- "Precious" items (metals, books, coins, or art)

Procedure
- Define decision criteria
- List and choose among alternatives
- Discover options and determine level of investment

D. Expansion Impacts on Consumer. When a firm increases: (1) quantity of goods or services provided, (2) the means of distributing these items or (3) the site at which the items can be obtained, then such firm outputs become more available for consumer use. In addition, higher-volume sales can mean lower unit costs which, in turn, can mean lower prices or more competitive pricing schemes. Third, advertising or promotion replaces word-of-mouth as the major means of reaching would-be consumers. However, as Exhibit 8-5 shows, there are added pressures in mass producing, distributing, pricing or communicating the firm's items. These pressures are to: i) standardize items or their distribution, ii) develop common ways of dealing with consumers and their problems and iii) construct uniform means of keeping track of goods or services volume. Item quality or variation will require careful planning to sustain a high reputation among consumers.

E. Expanison Impacts on Firm Makers. The larger the volume of standardized output a firm makes, distributes, operates, sells, advertises, or accounts for, the larger the number of members are involved with

Exhibit 8-5 Impacts of Expansion on Consumers

First-Order Effects

- Familiarity and informality being replaced with new faces and procedures
- Need for common guidelines directing interaction with consumers
- Pressure to have uniform accounting, personnel, marketing and production procedures to serve variety or volume of consumers
- Item "quality" needs greater emphasis and communication to existing and new customers or clients
- Not all of consumer's needs are served due to end items becoming less "customized" and more standardized

Second-Order Effects

- Move toward centralization of authority and decision making from "home" office
- Product or service information found through mass media (advertising or promotion)
- Less ability to serve consumer whenever consumer desires. Need for appointment or queue unless exceptional circumstances prevail

that output. That is, the percentage of uniform jobs greatly increases. Now, there may well be more opportunities to advance since there are more positions to advance into and, the gamut of benefits and incentives may widen due to more money available for them. Yet, the key indicators of member performance will be coordination and integration of all firm activities. That is, creative energies are put into sustaining better what already exists—that is, producing more rather than formulating some new item, process or scheme. As Exhibit 8-6 confirms, a stronger central authority and more uniform operating procedures are what could occur.

Further, the influence of large size can create a more impersonal, formal and rigid organizational climate unless steps are consciously taken by all firm members to reshape the organization to have more personal, flexible qualities in a larger operating environment.

F. Changing the Organizational Structure. At this point in the firm's evaluation, one basic question is: How well can the structure handle the business activities while satisfying member needs? The answer is to do an organizational audit to discover what functions need to be either strengthened or improved. Exhibit 8-7 shows some of the factors which can be audited as well as ways which the structure can be changed. Any modification would try to close the gap between directing and operating activities. Out of the modifications suggested at the bottom of Exhibit 8-7 could come from:

Exhibit 8-6 Impact of Expansion of Firm Members

First-Order Effects
- Requirement for policies concerning common activities at all sites
- Pressure to have prearranged, formal communication events
- Members no longer family or aware of all other members
- Personal concerns take backseat to performing specified firm activities
- Job variety and flexibility tends to narrow
- Roles and responsibilities become well-defined and hierarchical
- Clear limits to authority and means of delegating responsibility are spelled out
- Career advancement is well-defined and used as survival filter among members
- De facto emphasis on individual rather than team accomplishment
- Coordination and efficiency become more important than innovation

Second-Order Effects
- Rewards defined by organizational culture
- Informal communication becomes confined to immediate working group
- Shortest path to resolving problems may not be taken due to bureaucratic and political influences

Exhibit 8-7 Should the Organizational Structure Be Changed?

Factors to Consider
- Success in achieving firm's objectives
- Effectiveness of members' activities
- Viability of:
  - Communication patterns
  - Motivational incentives
  - Performance evaluation
  - Problem solving
  - Strategic planning
  - Control systems
  - Consumers served
  - Item quality, price, marketing activities
- Match between:
  - Job responsibilities and job skills
  - Job needs and their fulfillment
  - Job changes and their responses

Alternatives: Modify
- Delegation of authority
  - Way decisions are made
- Number of departments and how they are organized
- Kinds of jobs and how they are managed
  - Career incentives

- subsidiary arrangements;
- profit centers;
- nonprofit entities within the profit structure;
- more job autonomy;
- stronger group decision making;
- governance by committee;
- self-managing;
- managers who are problem or opportunity finders;
- looser structure with decentralized control;
- etc.

For these variations to be considered, there must be a strong desire to bring the structure more in line with the current business and member activities.

  G. Item/Pricing Scheme Alteration. Exhibit 8-8 gives the options one has for changing the outputs or prices once the size and kinds of demand are known. Other influences, as shown, all effect these important factors. But the insight noted here is not to decide on any item or price changes before the change influences are fully recognized and understood.

Sample Task 3

Come up with a means of accessing the impact of any pricing scheme alteration on:

Exhibit 8-8 Modifying the Firm's Items or Pricing Scheme

Observations
- There are four choices at any point during this stage:
  - Keep the product and/or service line and their prices unchanged
  - Narrow either item line or pricing scheme or both
  - Widen either item line or pricing scheme or both
  - Narrow one element and widen another
- Input which can cause change to items or prices:
  - Consumer acceptance
  - Consumer demand
  - Competitor activities
  - Local or regional development activities
  - Pricing patterns from nonrelated businesses
  - Marketing approaches or technologies which are performing well
  - "Production" costs generally or for each item
  - Contingencies

---

a. potential profit;
b. the existing pricing scheme;
c. consumer demand.

Which "principle" of pricing (simple, variable, complex, none, etc.) is likely to work best for you? Why?

H. Improving the Growth Plan. The thrust of strategic planning is to assist the firm to evolve to where effective managing of growth becomes a primary strategic issue. Here is where that strategic issue exists. Responding to it well requires focusing on what should grow, how fast it should grow, how it is re-related to the other firm activities and how it will be carried out and controlled. (These rudiments have been previously spelled out in Exhibit 6-14.) In addition, a growth principle needs to be articulated that firm members agree to and follow. (Example of growth principles were described in chapter 1.) Such a principle might be: We wish to grow well, not grow fast, since our growth is directed at long-term profit versus short-term market share. General and specific concerns to help carry forth a growth principle are found in Exhibit 8-9.

I. Influence Database Revision. Building on Exhibits 6-15 and 7-2, the suggestions made in Exhibit 8-10 are how to get the right kinds of information at the right time to members who need it. Besides improving the quality and timeliness of information, thought is appropriately given at this stage to developing an online database capability with an

Exhibit 8-9 Improvements to the Growth Plan

I. In general, the following concerns need to be discussed:

    A. Success of growth plan in achieving firm objectives

    B. Ability to resolve strategic issues through solving problems, handling contingencies and responding to opportunities

    C. Direction of growth is increasing firm viability rather than endangering its health

    D. Policy which clearly articulates the kind and rate of growth acceptable to firm members

II. In specific, address following concerns:

    A. Indicators which show whether level of growth obtained is acceptable

    B. Limiting factors to growth imposed by firm

    C. Conditions and accomplishments which must be satisfied before kind or rate of growth will change

    D. Alternatives to handle unsatisfactory growth

    E. Ways of monitoring implemented alternatives

    F. Contingencies and their impact on growth

Exhibit 8-10 Revising the Influence Database

Overall Discoveries
- Information which is crucial to firm operations and survival, gathered and used frequently
- Information which is useful but not essential to firm survival, gathered and used occasionally
- Information collected which has no or little application
- Inaccurate or incomplete information
- Requirements for new information
- Policies to direct information improvements

Specific Actions
- Discover the major information needs for each firm member, group, office, etc.
- Assess how well those needs are being met
- Evaluate how well the influence database is used to articulate strategic issues
- Prioritize strategic issues according to degree of urgency and impact. Either take immediate action, monitor continually, monitor periodically, take no action, or drop from consideration
- Give options to update and upgrade influence database based on overall discoveries and specific actions
- Choose, implement and monitor ways to sustain information which is available, useful, timely and instrumental as needed

optional network of communication terminals to assist in retrieving and manipulating the data. In addition, a data "housecleaning" would be effective in ridding the database of outdated, incomplete or inaccurate data or data no longer relevant.

Also, special studies are performed, as required, to augment the regularly received and analyzed information.

Sample Task 4

Discover how much information you need to stay in business. Find out how much information you are missing, not taking advantage of, don't have the evidence for, or not applying in new ways. What improvements can you make to the influence database procedures to get more impact from the information gotten?

J. Short- Versus Long-Term Success. Exhibit 8-11 portrays an accurate sense of what is involved with considering these time frames. Identifying realistic short-term and long-term time periods for the firm and thus

Exhibit 8-11 Trade-offs between Short- and Long-Term Success

Observations

- Degree of understanding of the differences and how each affects the other
- State company orientation—long term, short term, or neither
- Describe success and failure based on that orientation
- Articulate attempts to change firm orientation and prior results
- Discover how strategic planning helps or hinders the company orientation

Action

- Assess which orientation company should pursue
- Find out what steps need to be taken for pursuit
- Understand trade-offs among possible orientations
- Select time frame orientation
- Modify firm activities and operations to reflect new orientation
- Update strategic and contingency plans to reflect new orientation
- Monitor growth based on new orientation
- Strengthen firm activities to reflect success obtained

seeing which actions should be directed toward which time periods can greatly assist in defining and resolving strategic issues at this or any stage.

K. Obtaining Further Advice. At this point, you have interacted with inside or outside advisors or consultants (see Exhibit 7-13) and have used their recommendations to a greater or lesser degree. The observations stated in Exhibit 8-12 raised questions about how often to use advisors, how many to employ, how to choose them, effective means of communicating with them and how to direct their efforts toward a clear understanding of the problem or opportunity at hand and means to handle it. This can be an invaluable way to improve any facet of the firm as it evolves.

L. Reviewing Contingency Plans. In Exhibit 6-16, the definition and framework for contingency planning were presented. Here is a checklist that is used to ensure the contingency plans are operable, have been tested and are kept up-to-date. The actions required are shown in Exhibit 8-13.

Sample Task 5

How can you deal with new contingencies in better than a helter-skelter fashion?

M. Enhancing Member Relationships. As with the previous strategic issues, herein a checklist is presented for identifying deficiencies in member

---
Exhibit 8-12 Advisors and Consultants

A. Review
1. List all internal staff and external support received in last year.
2. Evaluate quality of interaction, usefulness of insights, impact on firm activities and current needs for more advice.
3. List strengths and weaknesses of advisors and strengths and weaknesses of your working with them.

B. Next Steps
1. Articulate means of overcoming advice weaknesses from firm members and for future advisors.
2. Describe ways to meet current advice requirements.
3. Decide how advice will be obtained.
4. Focus on getting information in a timely and useful fashion.
5. Note means of overcoming constraints to working with advisors.

Exhibit 8-13 Assessment of Contingency Plan(s)

I.   Evaluation
A. Number of contingency plans written, areas covered, means to mitigate impacts and resources required.
B. Past applications of contingency plans.
C. Results of applications.
D. Alternative ways of handling contingencies and their effectiveness compared to contingency planning.

II. Progress
A. Strengths and weaknesses of contingency plans.
B. Schedule of testing for contingency plans.
C. Modifications and updates based on past experience, present circumstances and future concerns.
D. Contingencies which will soon either be incorporated in strategic planning or handled by other means than contingency planning.

---

    relationships and ways to overcome them. Exhibit 8-14 should be used to uncover and resolve member frictions or misunderstandings which get in the way of effective relating as well as support ways to improve existing relationships. As with the other strategic issues, the sample firm situation shown below deals with improving member interaction.

N. Social Responsibility Plan. One of the major acts which is done to fulfill the definition of the firm is to carry out the mission (see chapter 3). In so doing, the firm consciously and directly contributes to the benefit of society. It has been said that just providing its primary output is a major contribution for the firm.

Exhibit 8-14 Enhancing Member Relationships

Investigate
- Breadth and depth of communication between members, among groups and throughout firm.
- Whether certain issues keep reappearing among members as important concerns.
- How individuals and groups handle personality or performance of other individuals and groups.
- What statements about the "relationship climate" can be made within the organization.

Action
- Obtain feedback from members about whether the relationship climate should be improved and, if so, in what ways.
- Achieve consensus on priority of relationship issues to be addressed.
- Discover alternatives to deal with these issues.
- Use decision criteria and select resolution pathways for all issues dealt within the short term.
- Implement resolutions and monitor impacts.
- Obtain feedback to sustain whether relationships are improving.

Yet, there are many members of society who cannot afford to buy the goods or services or there are needs that societal groups have which firms are not providing since they will not make a profit. So, in addition to the other concerns dealt with by the strategic plan at this stage, various areas where the firm can contribute to resolving or enhancing socially responsible situations are detailed. Exhibit 8-15 demonstrates how the members will focus on different areas, what specific options they will choose and how the options will be narrowed and carried out. The results of these "socially responsible" acts will enhance the firm's reputation, be the major way the mission will be accomplished and will be another important avenue for firm members to express themselves.

Sample Task 6

Do a cost-benefit analysis of potential socially responsible actions you can take. Do your findings suggest doing them? Why?

O. Reducing Waste, In Exhibit 6-13, the subject of how to keep costs down as activities rise was addressed. Cost control is one of the key areas for reducing "waste." Yet as Exhibit 8-16 demonstrates, there are other major areas which also need to be addressed to control unnecessary expenditures of resources, energy, effort or activity. The actions taken to rid the firm of wasteful practices are actions from which all

Exhibit 8-15 Plan for Social Responsibility

Inputs

I.   Firm Definition
    A.   Goals
    B.   Mission statement

II. Cultural Cues
    A.   Norms
    B.   Rituals
    C.   Symbols

III. Member Incentives
    A.   Benefits
    B.   Career advancement
    C.   Leadership

Options

I.   Environmental Preservation and Improvement
II.   Consumerism
III. Ethical Business Practices
IV.   Community Needs
V.   Business Philanthropy and Ethical Investments
VI.   Shareholder Relations
VII. Member Incentives Revision

Means

I.   Social Audit
II.   Strategic Issues
III. Past Actions

Process

I.   Strategic Alternatives
II.   Decision Criteria
III. Choice of Socially Responsible Actions
IV.   Implementation, Monitoring and Feedback

Results

I.   For Firm Members
II.   For Firm Reputation
III. For Society

Exhibit 8-16 Reducing Waste in Everyday Operations

- Identify Sources of Waste
  - Costs for materials, supplies, equipment, rent, leases, insurance, transportation, paperwork, telephone, computer, etc.
  - Time management of tasks including delegation, coordination, evaluation and responsive improvement.
  - Lack of effective problem-solving procedures.
  - Little or no control procedures or their failure to work well.
  - Excess of materials which are not directly useful.
  - Projects which are unproductive.
- Specify Means to Eliminate or Recycle Waste
  - Establish wiser costing schemes with suppliers, advisors, service companies and consumers.
  - Revamp cost centers to reduce overhead, activity and input costs through better control systems.
  - Redesign jobs and provide additional incentives to obtain and sustain minimum cost and resource operation.
  - Learn parts of business you lack knowledge in and integrate those insights into the rest of firm's operations.
  - Find ways to recycle waste from items provided or produced.
  - Discover sound means of managing projects to accomplish objectives and achieve resource and cost efficiency.

members learn to perform their responsibilities with more efficiency and effectiveness.

P. Handling Resistance to Change. The one constant which can be accepted with certainty as the firm evolves is that change will occur. Yet, change takes on different forms, lasts different times, and has differing impacts. If there are many changes, each with high-impact occurring simultaneously, a firm member can become overwhelmed by the change experience. Or, if the change is minor with short-lived impacts, the member still may reach similarity to the situation described in the last sentence. If, in either case or any change situation "in-between," a member or group of members should try to impede the change occurrence, its impacts or its implementation, the resistance must be noted and eventually dealt with. As Exhibit 8-17 points out, the process of resistance usually ends with the member or members trying to impede or prevent the change from occurring. The exhibit goes on to describe the means of overcoming the resistance by, in part, turning the same energy from resistance to cooperation. This "turning" occurs best through effective communication among the resistors or between the

Exhibit 8-17 Handling Resistance to Change

Process in Which Resistance to Change Occurs
A. Initial ill-feelings: hostility toward new person or action or activity.
B. Emerging dislike: feelings sustained as business activity progresses.
C. Trigger incident: threshold of discomfort reached and mind made up not to support change.
D. Additional influence: find corroborator to sustain your view.
E. Stonewalling: take actions to prevent change from occurring.

Means of Dealing with Resistance to Change
A. Acknowledge the resistance and its source.
B. Find assumptions behind resistance, noting that some resistance is healthy.
C. Come up with alternatives for overcoming resistance.
D. Select alternatives and specify who will monitor change action.

resistors and other members. Using Exhibit 6-11 can be a direct way of discussing the bothersome parts of change and what should be done to deal with those parts now and in the future The outcome of this incident could be a deeper understanding, respect and trust among all members involved.

Q. Overcoming Conflicts. Unlike resistance to change, a conflict can arise at any time. The process by which two people or groups come into conflict is based on:
  • difference in viewpoint
  • expectations
  • looking for a scapegoat
  • poor performance or interaction

As Exhibit 8-18 reinforces, when these ingredients are mixed together with the dose of "personality chemistry," a conflict is an unsurprising outcome. However, all is not lost. If the parties in conflict can still speak with each other then, informally, the tension can be resolved. If, on the other hand, neither party will speak to the other, then the means shown in Exhibit 8-18 can be used to resolve the conflict. With whatever measure is used, the guideline is to bring about an expedient yet fair settlement of grievances. Again, as with resistance to change, effective communication is the key to conflict resolution.

R. Learning from Failure. One of the seminal characteristics of successful entrepreneurs (as portrayed in Exhibit 3-3) is learning from failure. As Exhibit 8-19 clearly pictures, mistakes or failures are facts of business

Exhibit 8-18 Overcoming Conflicts

Germination of a Conflict

1. Preconceived notions: expectations about how others or he/she should behave.
2. Past experience: expectations are reinforced.
3. Thwarted ability: unrealistic expectations leads to poor performance or interaction.
4. Conflict inducement: attempt to cover up incident and/or stifle subsequent actions of others.
5. Conflict mushroom: tension and anxiety become focus of specific interaction. Both parties argue and possibly break off communication.
6. Stand-off: both parties are in mutually hostile state.

Means of Dissipating Conflict

1. Mediation: allow third party to assist those in conflict to arrive at consensus of settling the dispute.
2. Arbitration: allow third party to decide how dispute will be settled.
3. Committee resolution: have internal committee work through conflict with affected parties.
4. Self-initiative: one party recognizes incentive to resolve dispute with other party.
5. Power play: one party fires the other.
6. Adjudication: the dispute is settled in the courts.

Exhibit 8-19 Learning from Failure

First Step: Acknowledgement

- Describe the situation.
- Explain what went wrong.
- Discuss current status based on the situation.
- Articulate what insights were gained from doing and evaluating the situation.

Second Step: Prevention

- Give various means to stop the situation from failing.
- Demonstrate how the recent situation could have succeeded.
- Present a method for handling situations in the future to either turn them around or let them fail early.
- Use strategic or contingency planning to identify situations which need to be watched closely.

Third Step: Integration

- Provide incentives to have members show how they learned from failed situations.
- Encourage discussion of failure and ways to remedy it.
- Do not penalize failure for its own sake.
- Have topic of failure be included in training activities and growth plan.

life. The difference between one experience of failure and another is, however, the amount of learning which occurs to prevent future situations of this sort and to improve present circumstances.

Sample Task 7

Describe three incentives to stimulate learning from failure. Discuss how you would institute these. What impacts will the incentives have on longer-term member performance?

- S. External Opportunities and Threats.
- T. Internal Strengths and Weaknesses. T. & U. are discussed at length in the sample firm example shown below.
- U. Control Measures. Based on Exhibit 6-18, value control measures for this stage are shown in Exhibit 8-20 and are applied in the sample firm example given below.

Thus, the strategic plan for this stage is given in Exhibit 8-21.

STRATEGIC PLAN IN ACTION

This stage is where initial successes become the seeds from which the flowers of diversity blossom. The firm is instituting several added activities:

1. Classes for adults in dance and exercise classes for students and adults
2. Further discounts for various purchases

Exhibit 8-20 Using Control Measures in the Expansion Stage

1. Degree of goals achievement
2. Degree of mission accomplishment
3. Percent of market share
4. Level of member satisfaction
5. Degree of management style/individual leadership match
6. Level of integrating growth into firm functions
7. Effectiveness in handling resistance to change
8. Effectiveness in resolving conflicts
9. Change in output quality
10. Level of resource use efficiency
11. Soundness of economic and financial ratios
12. Degree of innovation

Exhibit 8-21 Strategic Plan for the Expansion Stage

I. **Firm Definition**

II. **Influence Database**

III. **Strategic Issues and Alternatives**
   A. Discovering more money
   B. Going public?
   C. Finding investments
   D. Expansion impacts on consumers
   E. Expansion impacts on firm members
   F. Changing the organizational structure
   G. Modifying the firm's items and pricing scheme
   H. Growth plan improvements
   I. Revision of influence database
   J. Short- versus long-term success
   K. Using advisors and consultants
   L. Assessing contingency plans
   M. Enhancing member relationships
   N. Social responsibility plan
   O. Reducing waste
   P. Resistance to change
   Q. Overcoming conflicts
   R. Learning from failure
   S. External opportunities and threats
   T. Internal strengths and weaknesses
   U. Control measures

IV. **Decision Criteria**

V. **Selection of Alternatives**

VI. **Implementation of Alternatives**
   A. Time table
   B. Summary of positive and negative attributes

VII. **Monitoring**
   A. Feedback
   B. Control methods

3. Enlarged line of "dance" products
4. Classes for handicapped and senior citizens in dance
5. Formation of student dance troupe
6. Providing free use of facility for community events
7. A dance lesson scholarship fund

The upshot of these actions is to require more people working more productively and with a spirit of cooperation and fun to make the additional hours put in worth it.

The first three issues in Exhibit 8-22 show various ways the firm can respond. Coplan and members decided to obtain as much needed capital from informal investors (friends, colleagues and associates); not to go public because control and direction of the firm should not be diluted; and to invest profits in different areas as mutually determined by members. Expansion has its impacts on the "personalized" nature of service provision. Responses as shown in Exhibit 8-22 mean members making every effort to consider the individual nature of each person instructed. The additional time spent can sustain consumer loyalty and possibly generate new ideas of conducting the business better. During this stage, the sense of business growth is turned upside down and inside out to find which means and resources are best suited to accomplish the expansion, now and in the longer term. However, the lesson from this effort is clear: grow according to plan and plan for later growth. Elizabeth Coplan is well aware that quick expansion can mean faster contraction and is not willing to let that happen. Instead, fine tuning of the strategic planning process is done to see that the right kind of information, possible responses, and ways of dealing with issues and implementation and control procedures exist and really work. And while the planning gets better, the relationships among members are explored and, wherever possible, improved as well (as shown in Exhibit 8-22). The time table for making the myriad of activities happen is shown in Exhibit 8-23. The eighteen-month time frame is chosen as a reasonable period—in which expansion can fully occur.

Measures of control are depicted in Exhibit 8-24. The controls at this stage are more general indicators of the total firm's abilities.

Finally, Exhibit 8-25 offers ways of dealing with the selected internal and external phenomena derived during the expansion stage. As with prior chapters, objectives for the next stage are determined at this point. Since we have made the assumption throughout that the previous set of objectives has been achieved, we will continue with that here also. The objectives for the crossroads stage of Coplan's School of Dance are likely to be as follows:

A. To establish a franchise operation and open six corporation-owned schools in the next fifteen months

Exhibit 8-22 Strategic Issues and Alternatives for the Expansion Stage of Coplan's School of Dance

Issue	Strategic Alternatives	Reasons	Comments
More Money	• Grant from arts organization • Private donations • Business supporters • Two equity investors	• Achieve objectives at this point • Meet accounts payable • Produce greater profit than previously • Positive impacts in short and longer run	• Start with profits have as capital • Work closely with accountant to efficiently spend money obtained
Going Public	• Decline • Do so in three months for amount equal to annual revenue • Do so in nine months for amount equal to four times annual revenue	• Provide additional incentive for members • Satisfy large fund in fusion requirement • Sustain financial viability • Boost demand for services and products	• Need to incorporate before issuing stock • Can dilute member's control
Firm Investments	• None • Other "socially responsible" companies • Money market funds • Paintings or sculpture of dancers	• Strengthen earning potential from profits • Want funds fairly "liquid" • Can do so on limited basis first • Members participate in investment decisions	

(continued)

Exhibit 8-22 (Continued)

Issue	Strategic Alternatives	Reasons	Comments
Consumer Impacts of Expansion	• All members willing to be helpers and problem solvers • Instructors have time for individual consultations • Members take phone calls at any time about any consumer concern • Ensure current enrollees receive firm information personally • Standardize procedures, not interaction or need fulfillment	• Counter impersonal feelings • Sustain high rapport with students and others • Hone competitive edge	
Member Impacts of Expansion	• Emphasize autonomous behavior and intelligent decision making • Set aside time for firm staff meetings each week • Strengthen orientation of new members with existing members • Stimulate new and better ways of conducting firm business • Members change responsibilities, not organization	• Prevent member alienation • Sustain self-improvement, leadership and willingness to get along • Fulfill firm definition • Better handle change	
Modifying the Organizational Structure			No reason to do so at this time

Issue	Strategic Alternatives	Reasons	Comments
Pricing Scheme Alterations	• Family discounts for classes • Student discount for products when become dance group member • Offer free samples of new products to see how they wear	• Encourage sustained participation • Increase cash flow • Hold competitive edge • Provide incentives for higher performance • Gage acceptance and growth of new classes and products	
	• Student dance group formed • Adult/student exercise classes offered • Design own line of exercise/dance wear and have current suppliers make it	• Reach larger local market • Penetrate regional market • Fulfill firm mission • Try improvements on limited basis first, then expand	• Hire three new members • Have two instructors be full time
Growth Plan Improvements	• Set aside time at every other firm meeting to address concerns of Exhibit 8-9 • Articulate ways to handle unsatisfactory growth • Have means to respond to contingencies such that they have minimum negative impact on growth • Develop procedure for reducing or holding growth rate if growth activities begin "running" members	• Problem prevention • Early opportunity advantage • Obtain as much benefit from growth as possible • Fulfillment of strategic planning	

(continued)

Exhibit 8-22 (Continued)

Issue	Strategic Alternatives	Reasons	Comments
Influence Database Revision	• Use Exhibit 8-10 • Decide which information is vital, which is unnecessary and which you don't have • Make effort to obtain right kind and amount of information from viable sources for timely usage	• Monitor availability of resources • Scan marketplace to discover how to provide services better • Improve member activities • Distinguish among public and private information	
Short- versus Long-Term Success	• Short-term actions and results are consciously directed to long-term viability	• Enjoy being in business • Desire new challenges and excitement • Want to accomplish new successes • Provide legacy for society • "Litmus" test of effective strategic planning	
Advice	• Make as much use of informal feedback as possible • Consider having an outside Board of Advisors	• No major concerns requiring specific help • Additional voices can provide additional insights about future moves	

Issue	Strategic Alternatives	Reasons	Comments
Contingency Plan Assessment	• Dry run existing contingency responses to see how they work for: fire drill, flood, power failure, bomb scare, vandalism, etc. • Ascertain additional contingencies to have responses for (i.e., failure for student to pay, sudden shortage of dance products, insurance cancellation, member accidents, etc.)	• Allow for minimal disruption of business or loss • Return to status quo quickly • Adapt to unforeseen situations • Have all members knowledgeable about required responses	
Member Relationships Improvements	• Hold retreat to air positive, neutral and negative perceptions, feelings and expirations about the firm • Take consensual actions to enhance communication, workflow, leadership, challenge and career advancement • Formulate procedures to deal with member resignation, termination, disability or death • Institute stronger ways of instruction and office management	• Fulfill firm definition • Improve working environment • Better respond to internal changes	

(continued)

Exhibit 8-22 (Continued)

Issue	Strategic Alternatives	Reasons	Comments

Social Responsibility Plan	• Define past and future responsibilities to consumers and society
	• Formulate actions to provide social benefits, such as:
	  - use of facilities for community events
	  - start scholarship fund
	  - give to charity
	  - hold benefits to raise money for charity
	• Ensure "culture" reflects ethical practices and ethical practices do enhance culture
	• Correct gaps between mission statement and actual practices
		• Enhance firm reputation
		• Provide increased demand
		• Demonstrates work style and lifestyle can be the same
		• Have positive societal results	

Waste Reduction	• Find sources of cost overrun and time overrun • Specify ways to reduce costs and time spent, including "recycling"	• Higher profit margin • More productive efforts • Ability to accomplish more or do it better in same time frame	

Issue	Strategic Alternatives	Reasons	Comments
Handling Resistance to Change	• Have one-on-one session to identify and deal with it • Discuss general phenomenon in regular firm meeting • Use third party if resistance becomes chronic • Have all members be trained in conflict resolution • When necessary bring in outside mediator	• Overcome constraints to productivity • Sustain problem-solving procedure • Validate individual treatment of this concern • Can negatively affect morale if lingers • Instance provides learning opportunity for all firm members	
Learning from Failure	• Each member describes periodically those actions which didn't work well. • Obtain feedback to achieve positive results in future • Members work together to correct failed aspect of firm	• Professional growth opportunity • Cease repetition of mistakes • Sustain, not lose, credibility with public	

(continued)

Exhibit 8-22 (Continued)

Issue	Strategic Alternatives	Reasons	Comments

Competitive Strengths and Weaknesses	• Growing, secure and well-balanced firm
	 • Providing greater diversity of services to wider array of consumer groups
	 • Costs have not sky-rocketed while space is efficiently used
	 • "Personal touch" retained in dealing with public
	   - Have not met dollar target for capital
	   - Quality of instruction has declined somewhat
	   - Members working to their time limits to meet all firm activities
	   - Space is used almost to the maximum
		• Effects on firm integration
		 • Importance of labor and resource utilization
		 • Ability to integrate growth with other firm activities	

Issue	Strategic Alternatives	Reasons	Comments

External Opportunities and Threats	• Building for sale nearby
	• Second dance studio has closed its doors
	• Schools will remain open
	• Supplier can manufacture dancewear cheaper than originally estimated
	• Franchise activity is up to 40% over last year
	  - Lease is up for renewal
	  - Parent considering lawsuit for her child's injury
	  - Competing dance studio now provides bus to pick up and drop off students
	  - Health inspectors found code violations. Order given to shut school down unless violations immediately corrected.
		• Means of satisfying expansion requirements
		• Long-term impacts of competition analyzed
		• Exploring options to be done incrementally	

Controls	• Use to effectively monitor successful integration of growth actions with existing firm activities	• Survival problems otherwise can occur • Used to handle minor concerns as they arise • Builds on application of controls from last stage	

Exhibit 8-23 Time Table to Reach the Crossroads Stage

Activity	Time frame											
	Month 1	Month 2	Month 3	Month 4	Month 5	Month 6	Month 7	Month 8	Month 9	Month 10	...	Month 18
Decide and Obtain More Money												
Make Firm Investments												
Resolve Impact of Expansion												
Change Service and Product Mix												
Alter Pricing Scheme												
Revise Influence Database												
Assess Contingency Plans												
Improve Member Relationships												
Institute Social Responsibility												
Reduce Waste												
Learn from Failure												
Handle Competitive Strengths and Weaknesses												
Handle External Threats and Opportunities												
Carry Out Controls												

Exhibit 8-24 Using Controls in the Expansion Stage

Control	Measure	Standard	Data Input	Interpretation
Degree of Goal Achievement	Number of goals accomplished divided by total number of goals	50%	Strategic planning output	By this stage's end, at least 50% of all goals need to be attained
Degree of Mission Accomplishment	Number of activities versus projected number	70%	Strategic planning outputs and member surveys	At least 70% of the mission is attained through this stage's activities
Market Share	Number of clients served divided by total clients involved in the area	20%	Internal records and external surveys plus public info	Minimum market share desired
	Firm revenue divided by total revenue of all firms in the area	30%	Internal records and external survey plus public info	Minimum market share desired
Member Satisfaction	Percent of satisfied areas for all work aspects	80%	Member survey	Minimum level to be experienced
Management Style/ Individual Leadership Match	Percent of inappropriate management decisions	10%	Member survey and discussions	Threshold beyond which match breaks down
Growth and Firm Functions	Number of growth problems which firm functions unable to handle	3	Member discussions and evaluation reports	Maximum number tolerated in a year's time. Yet, solutions for all problems need to be sought after
Handling Resistance to Change	Number of resistances outstanding versus total number dealt with	10%	Member discussions and records	Maximum percent which is allowed unresolved

(continued)

Exhibit 8-24 (Continued)

Control	Measure	Standard	Data Input	Interpretation
Resolving Conflicts	Number of unresolved conflicts versus total number which occur	10%	Member discussions and records	Maximum percent tolerated
Output Quality	Consumer level of 10% satisfaction now versus before		Student survey and historical records	Maximum difference in satisfaction allowed
Resource Use Efficiency	Change in dollars spent per supply or activity	10% decrease	Financial, accounting and marketing records	Minimum acceptable amount for higher efficiency
Economic	Revenue per student divided by cost per student	Various amounts	Financial, accounting and marketing records	Determine each to assess health of business
Financial	New students per marketing dollar spent			
Ratios	Revenue from product sales divided by revenue from dance			
	Total profit made divided by total debt payments			
	Net income divided by net assets			

Exhibit 8-25 Response to S.W.O.T.[1]

S.W.O.T.	Point of Discovery	Possible Response	Comments
Space Utilization	Class schedules— 95% used	• Consider expansion • Tighten schedule • Consider offering activities on Sunday • Expand hours of operation per day	
Capital Needs	Not met capital target by November 1 deadline	• Contact more prospects • Draw up plan showing specific uses of funds • Spread requirements over longer time frame • Raise money through promotional events	
Decline of Instruction	Student surveys Rise in number of complaints	• Hold retreat to discover whys of increasing instruction • Come up with effective means of handling complaints • Orient students at beginning of class • Deal with "problem" students sooner • Learn about new dance instruction techniques	
Member Workload	Hours of instruction per week	• Hire additional instructors full time • Hire additional part-time instructors and rotate staff • Discover ways to reduce time spent on noninstruction activities • Assign more noninstruction tasks to administrative staff	
Purchasing New Building	Instructor's friend owns it	• Project costs for staying in existing space • Discover financial aspects of purchase • Compare costs of staying versus purchasing based on services and products demand for next 5 years • Consider impacts of new location versus old	

(continued)

Exhibit 8-25 (Continued)

S.W.O.T.	Point of Discovery	Possible Response	Comments
Dance Wear Expense Reduction	Notice from manufacturer	• Increase promotion of dance wear • Begin mail-order operation • Become distributor for other area businesses • Start new subsidiary for students to sell to contemporaries and learn about running a business	
Parent Lawsuit	Letter from parent	• Discuss issue with lawyer and formulate responses • Initiate informal, in-person meeting to attempt to resolve concern • Take corrective actions to prevent student accidents	
Competing Studio's Transportation	Saw bus at studio	• Informally survey students and parents • If bus makes a difference consider providing van service • If bus will not make difference in student attendance than ignore	
Health Code Violations	Letter from health department	• Discuss with building owner • Respond with letter from lawyer • See health department officials and iron out discrepancies • Ensure that proper costs are allocated	

¹Competitive strengths and weaknesses and external opportunities and threats.

B. To boost the profit percentage per dollar of revenue by 12% over the next two years
C. To institute means to reduce member turnover and sustain consensual management style in new franchises over the next calendar year
D. To institute a new member training program so that productivity from each franchise rises by at least 15% from beginning to end of this year
E. To assure that consumer satisfaction will rise by 10% per year over the next three years
F. To establish an effective information transfer system among the franchises in the next year and upgrade it over the following two years

Also, any techniques or results from any previous stage or stage combination will be used to effectively carry out the strategic planning process in the crossroads stage.

Finally, the strategic issues which carryover from this stage to the crossroads stage are short- versus long-term success and growth plan improvements (since both are key to doing the franchising described in the next chapter); learning from failure and improving member relationships (based on outcomes of using controls); and the parent lawsuit. The reformulated strategic plan will thus be geared to strong survival with enlarged business activity and influence.

Chapter 9

Surviving the Crossroads Stage

SNAPSHOT

The firm has progressed to this point by overcoming some obstacles, responding to some contingencies and putting into practice a growth rate for sales, profit, resources and quality. The size, structure, consumer relations, firm member interactions and different activities have increased so that a new look is needed for continued evolution. This "look" is probably one of the most critical the firm will undertake, since the basic roots of its business activities will be assessed and the future shape, direction and working climate will be determined. The key activity of all members during this stage is not merely to do business or business on a different scale, but to do business while sculpting the future connections to allow the firm to survive for the longer term. In only two instances does the firm or its members not make it—organizational decline or member termination. All other situations are presented here with an eye to keeping the firm alive, progressing, changing and becoming a stronger and more viable entity. As with the other stages, the process to ensure the firm's survival is strategic planning. Exhibit 9-1 encapsulates the primary strategic issues likely to occur in this stage.

STRATEGIC ISSUES FOR THE CROSSROADS STAGE

This first part includes any or all of the new paths which a firm can pursue to attain stability, greater market success, better responses to changing conditions, stronger financial position, or a larger array of activities to pursue. The alternatives briefly described below in some cases are opposites and in other

Exhibit 9-1 Directing Strategic Issues for the Crossroads Stage

- Which new strategic activities will the firm pursue?
  - Joint venture   - Divestiture
  - Further diversification   - Retrenchment
  - Merger   - Bankruptcy
  - Acquisition   - Organizational decline or death
  - Partial or full sale of the firm   - Firm buyback
  - Buyout   - Franchising
- Who will do strategic planning and what changes, if any, will occur to how it is done?
- Which rate of growth is appropriate for this stage?
- How will the product/service mix and client/customer base be redefined?
- What procedures are there for correcting the chronic "ills" of the firm?
- What changes are needed to organizational structure and environment?
- How can firm members' abilities to adapt to change be enhanced?
- What options are there for career advancement and incentives to do so?
- How can the firm cope with member turnover including termination?
- When and how should the corporate culture be refined?
- What changes in founders' influence are likely to occur, and how should they be dealt with?
- How can controls and control systems be updated to be more effective?
- How must the management concept be altered during this stage?
- What competitive strengths and weaknesses will the firm face during this stage?
- What external opportunities and threats will the firm cope with at this stage?
- Which control measures are important for this stage?

cases can go together well. The lesson to be understood from reading the material shown directly below is to notice the interconnections among choices so as to choose alternative "packages," where feasible. Where not feasible, choose alternatives whose execution will use the existing firm resources to the greatest extent possible. (Do not assume, however, that another company's activities can be compatibly adjusted to your existing firm in a modular fashion. Actions from other places must be modified to suit the situation at hand, which can be risky.) The strategic choices indicative of the crossroads stage are, for example,

A. Joint Ventures. These can be undertaken by firms who find the resources of a corporation or partnership alone to be lacking and want, therefore, the "best of both worlds." The joint venture normally has two or more "parent" organizations who own the joint venture in common. Normally, the joint venture entity is set up for a special project or program, proceeds to complete that program and then either disbands or forms a more permanent relationship. From Exhibit 9-2, the profile

Exhibit 9-2 Making Joint Ventures Work

I.   **Reasons**
    A. Obtain project or program-oriented results
    B. Less expensive, in many cases, than mergers or acquisitions
    C. Do business overseas
    D. Do high-risk ventures
    E. Make resources available to firm not able to access in other ways

II. **Kinds**
    A. Enterprise agreements
    B. Research and development ventures
    C. Equity investments

III. **Types of Arrangements**
    A. Private—private
    B. Private—government
    C. Private—nonprofit
    D. Private—other, across national boundaries

IV. **Considerations in Forming a Joint Venture**
    A. Mutually assess ability to become "partners"
    B. Identify control and regulatory constraints to operations
    C. Specify division of responsibilities and outputs

V.   **Impacts**
    A. Cost savings due to economies to scale
    B. Shared overhead and know-how
    C. Common distribution network and other major factors as needed

of many joint ventures is, in many cases, either for "high-tech" start-ups or businesses in foreign markets.

Sample Task 1

How would you establish a joint venture with a marketing company to promote your product? Would this arrangement be more advantageous than merely retaining their services as consultants? Why?

    B. Further Diversification. After a certain "critical mass" of the firm is reached, further growth depends on spreading the current risks for the existing resources or fund expenditures. There are as many different ways to increase the diversity of firm operations as there are ideas plus one. The kinds of diversifications actions, their pros and cons and a decision about which are most feasible is required to pick the smart set of workable options. The alternatives, reasons and assessment factors are all given in Exhibit 9-3.

Sample Task 2

Exhibit 9-3 makes clear that there is a wide gamut of diversification possibilities. Assuming you decided to diversify, what technique would you use to decide among the degrees of feasible choices? How would you figure in risk?

    C. Merger. This strategic alternative is one of the most common carried out at a stage (like this one) where the firm is large enough and

---

Exhibit 9-3 Considering Further Diversification

I. Factors
    A. Time frame
    B. Degree of risk and liability
    C. Cost
    D. Expertise and coordination mechanisms available
    E. Impacts on initial firm activities
    F. Impacts on members and strategic planning

II. Reasons
    A. Firm outputs in industry approaching market saturation or obsolescence
    B. Outputs producing more cash than can usefully be reinvested
    C. Outcomes from research and development efforts
    D. Tax considerations
    E. Generate new business challenges
    F. Decrease vulnerability to cyclical, seasonal or other changes in demand, competition or firm performance
    G. Use excess capacity
    H. Fill new consumer need with existing resources

III. Types
    A. Related to primary firm activities or outputs
    B. Unrelated to primary activities or outputs
    C. Expansion of functions
    D. Expansion of outputs
    E. Expansion of market sectors or organizational buyers
    F. Broad or narrow increase in C. or D.
    G. General or specialized increase in C. or D.
    H. New businesses (subsidiary, profit center, franchise, etc.)
    I. Combination of A. through H.

well-established to find it beneficial to be involved with another company. Exhibit 9-4 displays the types of mergers and how one does occur. The purchaser of stock usually buys or trades at or above market rates or earnings/dividend rates. The time to merge can be in days or months depending on how soon qualified buyer/seller pairs can be found to merge and the process can be fully completed. In addition, mergers involve people, and without a conscious effort to build a rapport of trust and mutual respect among the separate parties, the eventual arrangement could have disagreements leading to failure to merge or major conflicts after the merger.

Sample Task 3

What circumstances would make merger the best strategic alternative to pursue of all those discussed in this chapter?

D. Acquisition. Unlike a merger, here one company will purchase the assets and liabilities of another company, causing that second company to cease to exist. (In the basic merger, the first company purchases stock instead of tangible items.) The primary concern about acquisitions are their ability to integrate one firm into the other and the way one company is approached by the acquiring firm. The second situation has become known as a takeover attempt. In Exhibit 9-5, the basics about acquisition are shown as well as how a company can prevent being swallowed up by another.

E. Partial or Full Sale. With joint ventures, mergers, acquisitions or further diversification the emphasis is on increasing the quality of firm activities. However, there may come a time when selling is preferred to buying a firm. The reasons and process are shown in Exhibit 9-6, noting that point under "Reasons" would use a modified "Process for Business Sale" as conditions warrant. The motivation to sell rests normally with the founders and is based on either change of lifestyle, career, or stated strategic objective. Your firm may be the one merged or acquired, but you can also sell some or all of the operations to a new entrepreneur. Also, the seller(s) need not wash their hands of all involvement. Provisions can be worked out for continued seller influence or activities.

Sample Task 4

List the major actions a seller must do for a successful partial or full firm sale. List the major actions a buyer must do for a successful partial or full firm purchase. How are the two sets of actions supposed to be similar? Why?

Exhibit 9-4 Carrying Out a Merger

I.   **Causes**
  A. Avenue for shareholders to achieve liquidity and higher stock profit
  B. Achieve higher efficiencies in access to and use of resources
  C. Become more competitive in pricing, outputs and response to changes
  D. Need for capital to fund growth since cannot obtain it internally
  E. Business no longer fits firm definition of strategic plan
  F. Reduce negative aspects of competition through merging with competitor
  G. Provide new outputs, sales volume, marketing channels and distribution networks
  H. Reduce tax obligations
  I. Present wider pool of effective management talent

II. **Types**
  A. Basic merger—Company A buys Company B stock, uses the assets and liabilities of Company B and it is discontinued
  B. Consolidation—Company A and Company B combine to form a third company, and then they are discontinued
  C. Subsidiary—Company A buys a significant portion of Company B stock with both companies continuing to operate as parent and subsidiary companies respectively

III. **Process**
  A. Discover "merger partner" who together can complement firm's past performance, current financial condition and future prospects of the merged business.
  B. Use proper third party to verify and consummate the merger.
     Generally, a merger consultant, investment banker or financial analyst is chosen.
  C. The third party develops a profile about the "seller" (firm who initiates merger) and compiles list of prospective "buyers" (firms who are convinced to merge).
  D. In addition, third party markets seller profile to buyer firms until buyer candidates are chosen by retaining seller identity as confidential.
  E. As buyers become interested, third party verifies their ability to execute the merger transaction.
  F. Those "buyers" who have degree of interest and are qualified will meet with "seller."
  G. Next, negotiations are conducted between seller and selected buyers.
  H. Merger completed with best-paired firms.

IV. **Effects**
  A. Could cause future job losses
  B. Avenue for super-bureaucracy and lowered productivity if done by large, staid organization
  C. Could cause value, management style and mission conflicts
  D. Without effective decision and performance control systems, merger will sustain lack of coordination and complete execution of strategic planning

Exhibit 9-5 Carrying Out an Acquisition

I. **Reasons**
   A. Completely gain control of a company's assets and resources without sharing management or profit
   B. Target company's stock may be selling for less than book value
   C. Target company may have a large cash surplus
   D. Organizational performance of target company is poor compared to its competitors
   E. Fast market penetration through purchasing existing firm with established reputation, clientele, production processes, resources and competent management

II. **Process**
   A. Carry out strategic planning to identify reasons why an acquisition would be done at this time.
   B. Construct profile of kinds of firm(s) which would be acquired
   C. Search and identify such firms in one or more industries
   D. Evaluate financial, resource and competitive potential of each firm as well as compatibility concerns
   E. Develop decision criteria and use to select two or three candidates' firms for "long-term" acquisition
   F. Conduct negotiations with each candidate
   G. Choose firm or talk with other companies or pursue some other strategic activity

III. **Effects**
   A. Acquisition activity can cause waste of money, time and productivity without creating new jobs
   B. Means are now devised to thwart "unfriendly takeover" bid, including:
      1. Change-of-control clauses becoming part of employment contracts of key executives
      2. Having board members elected to three-year terms on a staggered schedule
      3. Ensuring purchasing company will pay premium price for all stock it buys
      4. Leveraged buyout
      5. Corporate bylaws changed to require approval by high percentage of shareholders
      6. The firm being pursued makes a bid to acquire its pursuer
      7. A third firm is requested to acquire a firm subject to an unfriendly takeover
      8. Pursued or target company forces pursuer or acquiring company to seek regulatory agency approval
      9. Target company does divestiture or partial sale to make company value less attractive to pursuer
      10. Raise stock price, split stock or persuade stockholders not to tender their shares to offerer firm
      11. Other
   C. Acquisition may fail to integrate one company into the other, thus not achieving competitive advantage and cost-efficiency over developing acquired business internally

---

Exhibit 9-6 Selling Some or All of Your Company

I. **Reasons**

    A. Change careers

    B. Retire on proceeds

    C. Relinquish ailing firm or conglomerate

    D. Offer for your company too good to pass up

    E. Start new business with money from sale

    F. Founders no longer want to or are able to work together

    G. Business in stable or declining market

    H. Business or activity not contributing to firm definition

    I. Transfer company ownership internally to family, firm members, or partners

II. **Process for Business Sale**

    A. Determine worth of your company

    B. Demonstrate effective strategic planning

    C. Develop "buyer profile"

    D. Decide on influence, activities and incentives desired, if any, after the sale

    E. Be prepared to have seller conduct his/her own audit

    F. Use outside professional brokers or others as needed

    G. Locate several potential buyers

    H. Provide buyers with required information

    I. Tender offers and negotiate from buyers

    J. Accept offer, sign contract and assume or relinquish duties as agreed to

    K. Continue to search for buyer

    F. Buyout. This phenomena is relatively unique and rare compared to some of the other strategic alternatives just discussed. In this situation, specific designated parties buy controlling or complete interest in the company. These "parties" are, with one exception (outside investors), inside players in the firm. The thrust is that the management, leadership, strategic planning and financial control be retained by those already active in the firm. Buyouts are normally "private" transactions not subject to governmental scrutiny. And, one type of buyout is just the opposite of an initial public offering. Whatever the advantages and disadvantages shown in Exhibit 9-7, obtaining capital is a must. The "buyers" can offer a myriad of funding options, including upfront payment, equity interest, special interest payment arrangements, large lending fee, etc. Yet caution needs to be taken not to turn a buyout into a money well, since a strategic option of "flipping" the private company to another company or to the public made without proper business development can lead to a financial "blow out."

    G. Firm Stabilization. Besides the positive benefits of combining resources with another firm or selling some or all of the firm, there

Exhibit 9-7 Considering a Buyout

I. Types
  A. Business founder(s) bought out by other founder(s), executive(s), principal stockholder(s) or family
  B. Business subsidiary bought by operating managers and/or employees
  C. Public company becomes private company through executives, founders or outside investors purchasing public stock

II. Process
  A. Develop company profile for a leveraged buyout
  B. Founders, executives borrow funds from traditional lenders and/or contact one or more investors
  C. Obtaining required capital
  D. Discover potential buyers (lenders or investors)
  E. Present buyout procedure, benefits and company profile
  F. Qualify possible buyers, conduct negotiations, if necessary, and determine mix of buyers best suited to completing the buyout
  G. Consummate buyout and specify changes to operations, policies, planning and people

III. Advantages
  A. Less management or strategic planning interference from outside the company
  B. Ability to have long-term rather than short-term leadership
  C. Can lead to greater mission activities without need to explain each move to shareholders
  D. No reporting requirements to shareholders or Securities and Exchange Commission
  E. Owners have large stake in private company stock and thus have incentives to increase firm performance
  F. Company information is proprietary and less open to press or regulator scrutiny than with public companies
  G. Tax break from depreciating assets
  H. In certain situations, buyout can help firm avoid unwanted takeover
  I. Shareholders obtain revenue from stock sale which is, on average, 50% higher than market prices

IV. Disadvantages
  A. Founders, executives and/or members must concentrate on paying off new long-term debt from buyout, which can be up to 90% of total capital
  B. Limits expansion and growth due to large cash flow requirements
  C. In order to "cash in," buyout members will sell firm again to:
      1. Other firm
      2. Public
      3. Another buyout situation
  D. Lack of prior or present effective management practices or competent managers
  E. Key firm activities could be sold off soon after the buyout is complete

may come a time, particularly at this stage (though not confined to this stage), when the company operations or functions may have to be reduced, eliminated or redesigned. Exhibit 9-8 demonstrates what the causes are for putting stabilizing alternatives into place. The particular alternatives chosen depend on the severity and time frame of the downturn in primary indicators, yet, whatever actions are subsequently taken, the common objective is to bring the company back into a position where it can continue to grow. Further, the technique which makes this alternative important to discuss is early sensing. By this point in the firm's evolution, a control system needs to be in place to provide early warning of any situations requiring a stabilizing response. This "control system" comprises the influence database formation and implementation procedures for strategic alternatives. The watchword is, "the earlier the situation is sensed, the wiser the response can be to handling it." Finally, although downturns usually signal problems, they also could be precursors to discovering new opportunities.

Sample Task 5

What means would you use to handle stability situations before they occur, while they are occurring and after they have occurred? Would your actions be mostly similar, mostly different or some similar and some different? Why?

H. Bankruptcy. As shown in Exhibit 9-9, if a firm cannot pay its current obligations for any length of time, it can take one of two bankruptcy actions: either

1. Use Chapter 11 of the bankruptcy code to protect the business from its creditors while the members seek to reorganize its finances and reduce its debt.
   - Bankruptcy filings occur due to contingencies, overexpansion, undercapitalization, poor management or a combination of factors. If Chapter 11 is used, the following protections accrue to the troubled business:
     - Any foreclosure actions are halted pending an outcome from the bankruptcy court.
     - Creditors' lawsuits become void since debts owed will be resolved in the bankruptcy court.
     - Location evictions are stopped.
     - Other financial or material liabilities are frozen and handled within the bankruptcy proceedings.
2. Liquidate the firm's assets and closeout the business under Chapter 7 of the bankruptcy code.

Exhibit 9-8 Stabilizing the Firm

I. **Background,** There are primary indicators of a firm's well-being derived from the Internal Assessment (see Exhibit 5-3).
Examples include:
- Market share
- Profit
- Stock price
- Morale
- Level of assets
- Personnel or output turnover
- Productivity
- Record of safety
- Cash flow
- Sales volume
- Return on equity
- Earnings per share
- Degree of equity/degree of debt
- Costs of operation and their escalation
- Quality of output
- Amount of credit
- Number of members
- Break-even point
- Growth rate
- Resource allocation
- Pricing scheme
- Consumer quality services
- Etc.

II. **Types of Situations Requiring Stabilization**
   A. Retrenchment—a slight slowdown or sudden drop in one or more primary indicators
   B. Turnaround—a continual decline in one or more primary indicators over an extended period or a prolonged state of stagnation
   C. Random—a wide and unpredictable fluctuation in one or more primary indicators

III. **Courses of Action to Stabilize the Firm**
   A. Reduce the size or cost of operation
   B. Redesign the operation based on contracted size
   C. Reorient outputs to market including refining: line of outputs, target markets, applications to new markets, technical characteristics and/or pricing scheme
   D. Pullout of market and redirect resources to other activities
   E. After changes, continue modified operation until losses have stopped and growth can resume if so indicated
   F. Redefine jobs, responsibilities and incentives of firm members
   G. Divest company of unprofitable operations

Exhibit 9-9 Declaring Bankruptcy

I. Characteristics
   A. Reasons—varied but mainly lack of finances or education
   B. Types
      1. Chapter 7—liquidation of all assets
      2. Chapter 11—creditor payments and company reorganization to continue operations
   C. Time frame of occurrence—any time, but particularly first year of operation

II. Assistance
   A. Firm's attorney
   B. Bankruptcy court
   C. New sources of financing if required

III. Process
   A. Firm's attorney files petition for reorganization with the bankruptcy court
   B. Firm seeks new credit with priority payment arrangements
   C. Creditors committee formed to represent all creditors in specifying amount and time frame for full settlement
   D. Defaulted bank loans are considered and can be reinstated as long as regular payments occur
   E. Payments to Internal Revenue Service are priority but can be extended through negotiation
   F. Leases and contracts can be cancelled
   G. Concurrently, revamp and revise operations to be more efficient and cost-lean using strategic planning
   H. Sell nonproductive assets as source of capital. These are exempt from taxes for twelve months after reorganization plan is finalized
   I. Publicly traded corporation can issue new stock as another capital source
   J. Take revised strategic plan and convince and negotiate with creditors for acceptance

IV. Outcomes
   A. Dissolution of firm
   B. Sale to another party
   C. New start-up
   D. Sale of assets and new start-up

Thus, a basic reason for declaring bankruptcy is to prevent a secured lender from foreclosing. Yet, if you cannot show the court a willingness and ability to repay, and assist in obtaining credit or interest in settling your debts, the firm will be foreclosed.

Further, new creditors must be paid as bills fall due and will receive payments ahead of prefiling creditors should the business fail. No matter what advantages Chapter 11 gives a business, if there is no plan to make profits, the firm is likely to close for good within the next year to two years. Finally, bankruptcy is a means of being bought out by another company since it can obtain assets at less than market value.

I. Organizational Decline. Exhibit 9-10 summarizes the troubles which a company can experience and what are the causes of action open to resolve such longer-term problems. The litany repeated about poor management practices, lack of timely and sufficient financial resources, no strategic planning, failure to effectively take advantage of business opportunities, and so forth as given in Exhibit 9-10 is certainly true at this stage.

Exhibit 9-10 Organizational Decline and/or Dissolution

I. Sources of Decline
   A. Failure to change internal policies, procedures, and performance measures after they become inappropriate for current activities
   B. Inability to increase responsiveness to varying external events
   C. Lack of effectively resolving a major weakness or problem as organization matures
   D. Failure to establish and maintain legitimacy with consumers, lenders, investors, members, stockholders or society at large
   E. No or poor contingency planning
   F. Overcommitting resources to nonviable projects
   G. Short-term myopia blocking longer-term perspective
   H. Lack of appropriate management responses
   I. Poor financial planning
   J. Inappropriate application of strategic planning

II. Courses of Action
   A. Declare bankruptcy, rid firm of assets and close down all operations
   B. Declare bankruptcy, pay off creditors, reorganize and resume operations
   C. Correct downturn in one or more performance indicators
   D. Change leaders and ways of leadership
   E. Stimulate motivation of members toward higher performance and innovation
   F. Correct concerns in I.

But why do the founders, leaders, members and confidants allow situations in the firm to become a cancer on its survival? There are no general answers. However, there is a general insight-strategic planning, if done correctly, will tend to prevent concerns from becoming crises by requiring those involved to periodically deal with emerging situations. If these concerns are ignored or excluded from the strategic planning process, then the actions which ultimately must be taken are either ceasing operations, bankruptcy with reorganization or other major activities to reduce or remove "chronic ills" (as described below in Exhibit 9-16).

J. Buyback. This alternative has been used for many years but has taken on new respectability with the awakening to the new entrepreneur. In this case, the original owner(s) normally repurchase the company in order to turn around the company's operations and/or lead the firm in new directions. The advantage here is to obtain a company with a pool of underused resources and capabilities in conjunction with the leadership that started the firm. Exhibit 9-11 sketches the rationale for going forth with a buyback.

Sample Task 6

Discuss how you would plan to sell your company, only later to buy it back. Why would you do this? What impacts could these moves have on the long-term viability of the firm?

K. Franchising. This alternative may appear to be displaced in relation to the others previously shown because normally franchising is one means of new business start-up. Indeed, that is true. However, the new business becomes a franchisee. Here the discussion is about a franchisor—a firm which has achieved success and who wishes to package the operations, management, marketing and financing for other owners to buy in various locations. Exhibit 9-12 gives the basics to consider in deciding to franchise your business. The main advantage is achieving economies to scale by sharing the risk with other independent business owners. The major disadvantage is the inability to interest a large-enough segment of consumers to support your product or service. However, the best way to overcome this disadvantage is to have a "tried and true" item which you will first franchise experimentally, then later at full scale once the demand is proven and the operations are standardized and successful.

L. Updating Strategic Planning. At this point in the firm's evolution, the members can reflect on the fact that strategic planning has worked for

Exhibit 9-11 Buying Back Your Company

I. **Original Situations**
   A. Company merged with another firm
   B. Company acquired by another firm
   C. Major stockholder sells shares to existing owners
   D. Original owner relinquishes leadership role
   E. Company had leveraged buyout
   F. Company sold to new owners
   G. Firm in receivership or going through bankruptcy

II. **Reasons for Buyback**
   A. Keep firm from going out of business
   B. Alter and redirect firm definition
   C. Achieve level of success where others had not
   D. Have seller gain more than doing other options
   E. Economic viability greater than with other ownership

III. **Reasons to Sell**
   A. Business not profitable or well-matched enough to firm's short- or long-range objectives
   B. Original owner has know-how, familiarity, motivation and money to attain company solvency and growth
   C. Current owners will sell firm normally for less than paid for it and can usually obtain advantageous financing/equity
   D. Sell to capable turnaround personnel—original entrepreneur, former executive or current employees

IV. **Obstacles**
   A. Seller may change his/her mind
   B. Buyer may not meet seller's terms
   C. Buyer may only be able to purchase portion of original firm

the organization in charting its growth and development through proactive and interactive problem solving and opportunity exploiting. Yet, there may now need to be some modifications to the strategic planning process, who performs it, how the results are used, and incorporating more of its impacts on the firm's daily activities. The key question at this juncture is whether to formalize the process or expand the amount of member input given to it. In addition, other concerns include how sensitive the influence database is to detecting internal and external changes which may be critical to the firm's stability, continuity or innovation; and how directly the strategic planning results lead to making crucial decisions, responding to contingencies and solving major

Exhibit 9-12 Becoming a Franchise

I. Prerequisites
   A. Time frame of firm's existence
   B. Profit margin and financial ratios
   C. Growth of demand
   D. Competitors and their impact locally and nationally
   E. Degree of management expertise and capital reserves

II. Actualization
   A. Set-up legal requirements, financing package, standard operating procedures, resource requirements and training center
   B. Implement marketing method to attract potential franchisors
   C. Include extra services such as real estate, marketing, corporate incentives and other business development perks

III. Concerns
   A. Requires updating and reorienting strategic plan
   B. Could lead to large capital requirements to set up and expand locations of franchise
   C. Consider multiple franchises or multiple outputs at single franchise
   D. Start-up requires thorough and proper advice

firm concerns. The larger the number of basic activities which are handled outside the strategic planning framework, the less effective the strategic planning process becomes in providing options for future actions. Exhibit 9-13 summarizes the kinds of changes to consider for doing strategic planning.

M. Discovering the New Growth Rate. This issue has been of fundamental interest since chapter 6. Here, the growth rate is further refined (using the suggestions of Exhibit 9-14) to find which areas to grow in and to what degree. Based on past successes and failures and current potential activities, the growth rate with the largest net benefits for each activity considered will be found. These "rates" will next be tempered with availability of resources and people to choose the plausible rates of growth for each major activity (to be pursued in the next time period). Thus, by now, how much resources and how fast these resources will be used to obtain the desired output will be carefully assessed beforehand.

N. Refining Output and Consumer Mix. Along with strengthening the way a growth rate is found and used, the way outputs and consumers are matched and satisfied will be made stronger. Building on Exhibit 9-14, the factors to consider and actions to take in providing the right outputs at the right time to consumers are shown in Exhibit 9-15. If properly

Exhibit 9-13 Changing Strategic Planning

I. **Types of Changes**
   A. People involved
   B. Planning time frame
   C. Importance and time spent
   D. Resources used
   E. Control mechanisms

II. **Impacts of Changes on:**
   A. Involvement of principals in all major problem solving or opportunity making
   B. Communication inputs and outputs about strategic planning activities
   C. Work incentives
   D. Quality of outputs
   E. Future firm directions
   F. Consumer demand
   G. Ability to handle change and growth
   H. Member satisfaction
   I. Social responsibility of firm
   J. etc.

Exhibit 9-14 Finding Rate of Growth Appropriate to the Crossroads Stage

I. **Prerequisites to Discovering Growth Rate**
   A. Pace use of people, resources and coordination with growth so have proper utilization and effective management
   B. Understand range of growth which is plausible and doable
   C. Expand based on having right people for right jobs
   D. Describe activities you will do and will not do
   E. Discover the means to move quickly to close a growth "deal" if the situation warrants
   F. Have accounting and marketing control systems as tools to define and achieve strong growth rate

II. **Determining Growth Rate**
   A. Specify all growth activities which are feasible currently
   B. Calculate projected sales from each growth activity
   C. Compute costs and capital for each growth activity
   D. Develop alternative growth rates based on I.
   E. Assess impacts of each growth rate on firm well-being
   F. Choose growth rate with largest difference of positive to negative impacts on firm for each major activity

Exhibit 9-15 Redefining Output and Consumer Mix

Factors to Consider:
- Potential sales revenue
- Resource requirements
- Compatibility with existing "mix"
- Additional or new skills, techniques, processes, jobs, incentives, values and orientation needed to stimulate and satisfy demand
- Time frame for implementing "mix"
- External constraints and how to overcome them
- Modifications required controlling systems

Actions to Take:
- Build upon previous experience with items and consumers
- Penetrate market(s) at well-defined pace
- Improve existing product/service line based on results with new outputs
- Attempt innovative means of pricing, advertising and promotion
- Upgrade quality control standards, procedures and relationships among entire outputs set
- Streamline and reduce costs of operations wherever possible
- Emphasize member initiative in improving outputs provision

---

used, this exhibit will certainly reflect a firm where member desires and actions and firm functions and results work well together in getting closer to achieving firm goals.

O. Resolving "Chronic Ills." Most companies by this stage have either a series of special projects which are ongoing or a group of internal staff or consultants whose task is to devise and implement results from special projects. One such project might be what is portrayed in Exhibit 9-16. Here, those internal weaknesses or external threats (or other problems) which have been with the company either from inception or for several strategic planning cycles are at last directly addressed, evaluated and resolved. Although these chronic ills may have had little negative impact on the firm's activities up until now, resolving these problems can rid the firm of obstacles to better channeling the resources and energies of the firm.

Sample Task 7

Identify five chronic ills. Specify how you will "cure" them. Can they be totally eliminated? Why?

P. Improving the Organization. This important stage is also one for firm "house cleaning." As Exhibit 9-17 shows, the company can do

Exhibit 9-16 Correcting "Chronic Ills" within the Firm

I. **Sensing and Identification**
   A. List past problems or weaknesses which have carried over beyond one stage in the firm's evaluation and are still unresolved
   B. Summarize efforts to take care of these concerns
   C. Delineate and discuss reasons why problems or weaknesses still exist
   D. Present current efforts, if any, to deal with these concerns

II. **Alternatives Generation**
   A. Come up with the means to completely handle problems using several methods. For example:
      1. Group(s) brainstorming session
      2. Retreat to find answers and workable means to eradicate concerns
      3. Incentive contest for creative/workable solutions
      4. Research project to find root causes and how they are to be handled
      5. Outside assistance along with 1-4
   B. Hold open firm meeting to present ways of correcting chronic ills
      Ask for feedback, constructive criticism and further suggestions

III. **Implementation Pathways**
   A. Designate special person(s), group, committee, etc., to oversee and actively participate in putting solutions into action
   B. Ensure special person or group obtains feedback, does monitoring and carries out quality control
   C. Discuss applying this technique to nonchronic concerns

Exhibit 9-17 Improving the Structure and Environment of the Organization

I. **Do they need improvement?**
   A. Specify small number of "internal" consultants to gather insights, feedback and assessment about the effectiveness of the structure and health of the working environment from all firm members
   B. Evaluate the responses and produce "wish list" of potential positive changes
   C. If no changes are suggested, discover why and find out what new activities could enhance the existing ones

II. **How and when will such improvements occur?**
   A. Develop priority among possible actions
   B. Use decision criteria to select those actions which can be done within resource limitations
   C. Produce time table and task order for all selected actions
   D. Implement, monitor, improve and control changes to structure and working environment in relation to strategic activities
   E. Prepare to influence longer-term impacts of changes on firm's definition and activities

a thorough review of the way the structure operates and diagnose the health of the working environment. Based on the discoveries from these undertakings, a set of improvements are produced for each area. As with previous discussions in this chapter, the implementation and monitoring of such improvements is an important way the firm can effectively position itself internally for long-term viability.

Q. Stimulating Career Options for Members. Closely in conjunction with Exhibit 9-17, the firm members can also assess their satisfaction and career motivations with the firm. In so doing, the rest of the "behavioral concerns" (as shown in Exhibit 9-18) can be addressed. From these impressions and facts, the members can directly discover and make the needed changes to enhancing their interaction, influence, and innovation toward long-term satisfaction.

Sample Task 8

What three vital characteristics of your firm would retain members for the long term? Do you have these in practice currently? Are members wanting to stay? What can stimulate their desire to continue to be firm members?

R. Coping with Member Turnover. No matter what degree of sensitivity or number of actions are taken to involve members with their future in the organization (as shown in Exhibit 9-18) it is inevitable that some members will leave, be terminated or stop work for other reasons. The issue of turnover is key since how the firm responds to individual members is a litmus test of the consistency between talk and action. Whatever reasons occur for member turnover (as given in Exhibit 9-19), it is vitally important that the membership of the organization use the "leaving experience" as a means to strengthen existing member relations. This action can occur through obtaining feedback from the former member to stimulate improvement discussions. Also, having procedures on hand to assist the member in his or her next job and/or personal situation could sustain the benevolent value of the firm and lead to referrals of qualified, potential members. Finally, should a dispute over termination arise, both the former member and firm member representative(s) can informally, expeditiously and equitably resolve it. One of the best ways to grow is to learn. Member turnover is an excellent time to learn both what went right and what can be done better.

S. Updating the Corporate Culture. As with the other internal facets of the firm, the corporate culture, too, needs reassessment. A "template"

**Exhibit 9-18 Enlarging and Enhancing Career,
Change and Incentive Options of Firm Members**

I. **Existing Situation**
   A. Have member working group put together means of obtaining feedback from firm members on career, change and incentive options
   B. Gather information on these topics
   C. Compare information with current firm actions to note discrepancies and inconsistencies with:
      1. Goals and objectives
      2. Values
      3. Leadership
      4. Communication
      5. Impacts of incentives on motivation
      6. Stress, conflict or resistance to change
      7. Group behavior
      8. Productivity
      9. Member turnover
      10. Problem solving/decision making
      11. Advancement procedures
      12. Participation in strategic planning and review of firm's accomplishments
      13. Satisfaction with and assistance from incentives
      14. Other
   D. Summarize findings in terse document which all members receive

II. **New Situation**
   A. Hold retreat, workshop, conference, etc., to address findings in part I.D.
   B. Brainstorm and refine options for rectifying situations at the individual, group and firm level
   C. Based on ranking of options, pick those of vital concern
   D. Assess and specify resource requirements, procedures and logistics to implement vital options completely and soon
   E. Show what monitoring will do to ensure strong options move beyond ideas to actions

for carrying out this reevaluation is given in Exhibit 9-20. The objective here is to discover in what way can the culture acquire additional practical use and be more reflective of the changing values of firm members.

Sample Task 9

Describe your firm without a corporate culture. Is anything of value missing? If so, can it be replaced some other way?

Exhibit 9-19 Coping with Member Turnover

I. External Reasons
   A. Better job opportunities elsewhere
   B. Better working environments within other companies
   C. Fast growth of industry creating much demand for particular skills
   D. Potential decline in demand among firms in industry

II. Internal Reasons
   A. Declining work environment in terms of responsibility, participation, career advancement, interaction, incentives, culture, etc.
   B. Decreasing emphasis on work quality, job satisfaction, learning new skills or from failure, or responding well to changing conditions
   C. Inappropriate or unethical business practices
   D. Failure to effectively respond to contingency
   E. Requirement to reduce and consolidate member force
   F. No provision of career advancement pathways

III. Personal Reasons
   A. Requirement for geographic move
   B. Increasing personality friction with firm members
   C. Lack of strong performance
   D. Health concerns of member or family
   E. Sense of widening gap between personal and organization goals
   F. Declining desire to contribute to organization
   G. Desire to change career position

IV. Options
   A. Member resigns, retires, takes leave of absence, or transfers to sister of related company
   B. Member is laid off
   C. Member is fired
   D. Member given health termination

V. Assistance from Firm
   A. Continued benefits as situation warrants or previously agreed to
   B. Help in finding another job
   C. Consulting relationship until employed again in full-time position
   D. Debriefing and resolving behavioral concerns

VI. Assistance from Member
   A. Communication with other members about situation
   B. Completion of any outstanding projects
   C. Observe priority nature of products, patents, information and turn over all such documents

VII. Dispute from member (if deemed necessary)
   A. Protest to the firm founders
   B. Informal legal inquiry from member lawyer to firm lawyer
   C. Formal legal investigation
   D. Legal hearing by impartial committee, mediator or arbitrator
   E. Legal suit brought against company

Exhibit 9-20 Refining the Corporate Culture

I. Why
   A. Values out of phase with practices
   B. Rituals and symbols increasingly meaningless among firm members
   C. Culture is ignored or countermanded by members
   D. Improve "way things are done around here"
   E. Culture is not well-received among public groups
   F. Lack of clear, firm definition

II. When
   A. During strategic planning sessions
   B. Before implementing strategic alternative
   C. After responding to contingencies
   D. Subsequent to some major change in the firm previously planned

III. How
   A. Have group think session, all-day retreat, facilitated organization improvement workshop, etc.
   B. Discover specific ways culture is nonreflective of members' needs and firm activities
   C. Brainstorm many means to bring culture in-sync with organizational directions and member motivations
   D. Involve members in selecting and implementing alternatives to strengthen culture
   E. Have periodic "culture monitoring" to strengthen cooperation and innovation among firm members

   T. Redefining the Founder(s) Influence. From the "get-go," the founders have put in a combination of energy, insight, foresight and skills to bring the firm to what it is today. These individuals are to be credited for accomplishments and have motivated others to strive for similar levels of achievement and satisfaction. The founders have sculpted the culture, created the ideas for the outputs and been the "rudder" to guide the firm through difficult times and crises, in taking risks, and in effectively sharing the fruits of success with members, shareholders and society. At this stage, founders are, in many cases, rethinking their present and future role and influence with the firm. There are many routes these thoughts can take.

Exhibit 9-21 Redefining the Founder(s)' Influence

I.   Major Aspects of Influence
  A. Generated initial idea for company
  B. Started, achieved success and expanded company through, in part, their leadership
  C. Vision of firm definition is guiding light for organizational culture
  D. Values direct how business is done and what new activities and innovations can occur
  E. Provide motivation to have ongoing strategic planning process
  F. Direct contributions made to society by firm members

II.   Shortcomings to Influence
  A. Unable to achieve full potential of company
  B. Not capable of effectively responding to changes
  C. Personality or values limits amount of satisfaction members can derive
  D. Personal concerns adversely affect management style or leadership
  E. Do not possess skills to run diversified organization

III. Means of Modifying Founder(s)' Influence
  A. Replacing founders with outside managers
  B. Reducing founders' role and using inside personnel to do tasks relinquished
  C. Expanding founders' influence but reducing founders' authority
  D. Carrying out succession plan (see Exhibit 9-22)
  E. Defining new role for founders

Exhibit 9-21 provides some direction on which changes in emphasis the firm founders may wish to pursue. The level of involvement, final authority, personal resources, benefit (short and long term), and future leadership are prime facets for consideration. Where needed, outside corporate managers can bring professional competency to managing a diversified organization.

U. Planning for Succession. One major concern founders have at this point is whether and when succession should occur. Exhibit 9-22 portrays what is involved in putting some forethought and procedures together for selecting "up and coming" members for career advancement to large levels of responsibility and/or family members to areas of key influence.

V. Updating Controls. One of the main reasons that the firm succeeds is based on effective controls and the control system which the firm implements. As discussed in previous chapters (specifically, Exhibits 5-21, 6-15, 6-19, 8-9, and 8-13), control mechanisms are central to effective implementation of strategic actions. Yet, in evaluating how

Exhibit 9-22 Planning for Succession

I. Reasons
   A. Ensure continuity of firm activities and longer-range survival
   B. Keep disruption of leadership, innovation and strategic planning to a minimum
   C. Have current leaders, founders and members give input as to who successors may be
   D. Provide career advancement pathways
   E. Reduce member turnover
   F. Provide contingencies in case health or catastrophe should prematurely limit founders' longevity with firm

II. How It Is Done
   A. Informally—through positing what kind of management and other skills as well as attitude will be needed by people with a lot of influence in the organization. Then, work backward to discover what training and experiences current members need to have to become future leaders.
   B. Formally—institute system to select and train potential successors. Career development inventories are written for high-potential candidates and along with previous performance appraisals are used to produce succession "strategic plan" in specifying ways to increase strengths and reduce weaknesses. This talent pool is compared with projected jobs, responsibilities and strategic actions to ascertain when and how each person will be fulfilling future positions.

III. Advantages
   A. Assists in discovering members with high growth potential
   B. Improves performance evaluations to emphasize what person does first and who he/she does these things for second
   C. Gives fair means of selecting members for larger levels of responsibility, influence and achievement
   D. Puts less pressure on firm to bring in leadership capability from the outside
   E. Gives impartial procedure for involving family members eventually in positions of key influence to firm's subsequent directions

IV. Disadvantages
   A. Succession planning controlled and dictated only by founders
   B. Failure to link succession planning to strategic planning
   C. Founders set up procedure and then choose successors based on nonrational criteria

---

Exhibit 9-23 Updating Controls and the Control System

I.   Status Evaluation
    A. Examine current controls and their procedures
    B. Determine strengths and weaknesses of control systems
    C. Discover control "gaps"—areas where controls are needed

II.   Next Steps
    A. Suggest ways of upgrading and strengthening control procedures across **all** major firm activities
    B. Prioritize control actions
    C. Develop implementation schedule
    D. Monitor control procedures to ascertain whether they are effectively operating
    E. Ascertain impacts of strengthened controls on productivity, outputs, achievement of firm objectives, member satisfaction, ability to respond to change, etc.

---

successful the actions were in furthering the firm's definition, glitches, mistakes and gaps are likely to be uncovered in the control procedures. Exhibit 9-23 shows how to correct the control system to be even more powerful in monitoring the individual firm activities and their mix.

W. Altering the Management Concept. The present and future status of firm managers is assessed at this point. The definition of what management now comprises in the company, who are the firm's managers, what functions managers should perform and how founders and managers should relate need to be clarified. Exhibit 9-24 describes further the changes possibly needed to strengthen the managerial functions as the firm enters a longer-term survival period.

Sample Task 10

Evaluate this notion: At this point in the firm's evolution, management is no longer required since all managers are workers and all workers are managers. Does this make sense in terms of strong strategic planning toward the next stage?

X. and Y. Examining Competitive Strengths and Weaknesses and External Opportunities and Threats. As in the previous chapters, the actual firm example will summarize the strategic issues in this format.

Z. Measuring Control. The specific controls connected with this stage are shown in Exhibit 9-25. They are comprehensive and reflective of the overall firm progression.

The overall strategic plan for the crossroads stage is shown in Exhibit 9-26.

Exhibit 9-24 Altering the Management Concept

I. **Current Situation**
    A. Kinds of managers
    B. Basic duties and functions
    C. Degree of authority
    D. Centralization of decision making
    E. Problems with management activities, reception by other members and success of the firm
    F. Types of members, their jobs and degree of contribution to firm definition

II. **Possible Changes**
    A. Relationships between founders and managers
    B. Relationships between managers and other firm members
    C. Emphasis on delegation and decentralization of authority and decision making or its opposite
    D. Expansion of manager duties or its opposite
    E. Increased contributions to organizational culture, strategic planning and member development
    F. Kinds of firm members for future organization

Exhibit 9-25 Measuring Control during the Crossroads Stage

- Controls
- Degree of firm solvency
- Compatibility of activities mix with organizational definition
- Degree of member adjustment to changes
- Effectiveness of organization for long-term survival

STRATEGIC PLAN IN ACTION

Coplan's School of Dance has decided at this juncture to proliferate the dance school design in franchise form. After many discussions with nondance and dance franchisors and franchisees, the firm developed the strategic plan to open and expand on a franchise basis. This means determining what the output mix will be at each site, where the sites will be, what pricing scheme to be used, who will manage or control or test at the selected sites, what the options are given for the performance results, and how the franchise arrangement will operate. Given that franchising becomes the major thrust during this time period, the members are now faced with absorbing changes to: the organizational structure and environment, handling member turnover, the founders' influence, the management concept, accounting and marketing for the firm, and member relationships and advancement. Most of all, the members need to

Exhibit 9-26 Strategic Plan for the Crossroads Stage

I.   **Firm Definition**

II. **Influence Database**

III. **Strategic Issues and Alternatives**
   A. Strategic Alternatives
      1. Joint Ventures
      2. Further Diversification
      3. Merger
      4. Acquisitions
      5. Partial or Full Sale
      6. Buyout
      7. Firm Stabilization
      8. Bankruptcy
      9. Organizational Decline
      10. Buyback
      11. Franchising
   B. Updating Strategic Planning
   C. Finding the New Growth Rate
   D. Refining Output and Consumer Mix
   E. Resolving "Chronic Ills"
   F. Organizational Improvement
   G. Career Options for Members
   H. Coping with Member Turnover
   I. Updating the Corporate Culture
   J. Redefining the Founder(s)' Influence
   K. Succession Planning
   L. Updating Controls
   M. Management Concept Alteration
   N. Examining Competitive Strengths and Weaknesses
   O. Examining External Opportunities and Threats
   P. Measuring Control

IV. **Decision Criteria**

V.   **Selection of Alternatives**

VI. **Implementation of Alternatives**
   A. Timetable
   B. Summary of positive and negative attributes

VII. **Monitoring**
   A. Feedback
   B. Control Methods

be concerned with establishing an effective rate of growth (using Exhibits 8-9 and 9-14) that will give leeway to respond to contingencies while providing directions for long-term stability and success. Oh, and while they're at it, the members need to seek to eliminate chronic problems or inefficiencies.

As previously shown, the firm's strategic alternatives are provided in Exhibit 9-27, the time table for successful franchising given in Exhibit 9-28, control measures used for the firm as a whole shown in Exhibit 9-29 and selected internal/external concerns and their cures prescribed in Exhibit 9-30.

There are no new objectives specified here since in the next stage, the entire definition of the firm will be redone. Yet, any techniques or results from prior stages which may be useful in the maturity stage should be so stated and applied.

Finally, the strategic issues which carry over from this stage to the maturity stage are franchising, refinement of outputs, and improvements to the work environment (since all issues are primary to the practice and projects done in the next stage). Long-term survival, firm solvency and firm process/behavior match are controls which indicate further strengthening of these facets during the next stage. The reformulated strategic plan is now centrally directed toward balancing new, creative efforts with stable, long-term successes.

- Divestiture
- Retrenchment
- Bankruptcy
- Organizational decline or death
- Firm buyback
- Franchising

Exhibit 9-27 Strategic Issues and Alternatives for the Crossroads Stage of Coplan's School of Dance

Issue	Strategic Alternative(s)	Reasons	Comments
Franchising Consummate	• Establish franchise corporation • Open franchises owned by corporation in Washington, Baltimore and Richmond metro areas • Gage and monitor success • Iron out franchise "bugs" • Decide on whether further expansion will include franchisors, remain company owned or both	• Long-term viability of company • Innovate new concept • Can implement on limited basis first • If unsuccessful, can return to status quo • Build on previous experiences	Action with strategic plan Franchising contingent on member acceptance and support
Strategic Planning Changes	• Have revolving committee who formulates and direct changes to strategic plan(s) • Plan(s) approved by member consensus • Identify changes through "audit" procedure	• Ensure member participation • Sustain expertise among all firm members • Open to new insights and techniques for improving strategic planning	
Outputs Refinement	• Set up means to balance existing business with new franchise activities • Redefine pricing, marketing and quality controls • Identify new skills, processes, jobs, incentives and coordination means to satisfy increased demand	• To sustain firm definition • To enable firm to grow at sane pace • To successfully meet new challenges • To effectively and quickly handle adverse responses • To sustain highly visible reputation	

Issue	Strategic Alternative(s)	Reasons	Comments
Chronic Ills Correction	• Marketing methods strengthened • Administrative services coordination improvement • All-day seminar to determine other areas for correction	• Stop internal mismanagement • Provide additional areas for member contributions • Prerequisite to effective expansion	
Organizational Structure and Environment Improvements	• Discover ways to ensure effective replication of "consensual management" style in each franchise • Develop coordination procedures among franchises that work • Redefine communication, career advancement, consumer interface, incentives and culture in light of franchise expansion	• Need organization with equally strong autonomy and cohesiveness that are compatible together • New jobs, functions and responsibilities require new perspective on work, objective attainment and advancement • Eliminate potential sources of consumer or member alienation	
Member Turnover	• Establish procedures for resignation, termination, disability or death • Improve performance evaluation procedures • Agree on means to deal with unethical member behavior • Develop ways of sensing dissatisfactions early • Broaden member growth possibilities to include leave of absence • Strive to have growth opportunities herein be better than any competing firm • Improve hiring and acclimation methods	• Reduce frequency and amount of "unnecessary" turnover • Achieve member consensus and action on coping with turnover • Coordinate solutions with all other facets of internal environment • Reduce costs and productivity loss of workforce • Provide holistic basis for members to stay and grow • Improve abilities to deal with change	

(continued)

Exhibit 9-27 (Continued)

Issue	Strategic Alternative(s)	Reasons	Comments
Founder(s)' Influence Refinement	• Putting together a succession plan for Elizabeth Coplan and other early members • Identify limits to influence and shortcomings • Come up with means to strengthen and expand member influence as franchises increase	• Cannot afford to lack business operating skills • Require assistance, support and leadership to achieve expansion successfully • Bringing in or training stronger leaders paves the way to long-term survival • Discover what future role(s) of early members will be	
Management Concept Alteration	• Redefine management tasks all members do • Specify activities certain individuals do • Discover "range of self-governing" members desire • Reassess how authority gets defined and delegated • Rebalance individual versus organizational goals	• Give justification for future management style • Describe attitude toward strategic planning, business at ions and each other • Discover linkages between a strong financial picture and a strong behavioral picture in the firm • Explicate interaction with consumers as reflection of member interactions	

Issue	Strategic Alternative(s)	Reasons	Comments
Competitive Strengths and Weaknesses	• Highly successful coordination of multisite operations • Sharing of ownership with new franchisors • Strong financial performance • High public acceptance and media promotion • Correction of administrative and marketing weaknesses - Barely enough money to finance franchise operations - Lack of full vocational survey before opened new dance schools - No change in name of firm - Frictions created between old and new members - Failure to apply strategic planning to start-ups	• Built on prior experience, strategic planning and growth • Fulfill firm definition • Prove innovative concept successful • Pressures for immediate results • Fast expansion of membership occurring • Consider new locations as additional pieces of old "pie" rather than new "pie"	
External Opportunities and Threats	• No competition for this concept • Youth looking for new ways to channel energies other than in video games • Emphasis on more family activities • Public wants to participate close to home, at convenient hours, in good surroundings, with proper exercise, at various levels of commitment which are of low cost	• Designed expansion to carve out unique niche • Appeals to artistic and exercise needs simultaneously • Provide consumers with environment to channel energies • Need to respond to other competitors • Willing to risk not building own facilities or manufacturing plant	

(continued)

Exhibit 9-27 (Continued)

Issue	Strategic Alternative(s)	Reasons	Comments
	• Amount of leisure time continues to grow - Competition *now* from "non dance" leisure activities - Leases can be revoked or not renewed - Possible dance wear shortage - Insurance costs are rising rapidly - Demand outpaces ability to supply services and products	• Firm controls demand	
Controls	• Use prior controls to monitor firm means and ends • Introduce new controls reflective of overall firm achievement and solvency • Upgrade controls to reflect new environment	• Crucial for effective assessment of performance	

Exhibit 9-28 Time Table to Reach Maturity Stage

Activity	Time frame										
	Month 1	Month 3	Month 5	Month 7	Month 9	Month 11	Month 13	Month 15	Month 17	Month 19	... Month 36
Develop franchise concept	———										
Implement and test franchise			———								
Make improvements and describe franchise expansion plan				———							
Implement plan								———			
Open new school					———						
Sustain effective coordination							———				
Solicit franchisors and award rights					———						
Integrate all franchise activities									———		
Sustain self-management and consensual style					———						

(*continued*)

Exhibit 9-28 (Continued)

Activity	Time frame											
	Month 1	Month 3	Month 5	Month 7	Month 9	Month 11	Month 13	Month 15	Month 17	Month 19	...	Month 36
Correct chronic ills and deal with member growth needs								—				
Agree on contingency responses concerning members and original members					—							
Cope with competitive strengths and weaknesses			—					—	—			—
Cope with external opportunities and threats				—		—			—	—		
Carry out controls			—									—

Exhibit 9-29 Using Controls during the Crossroads Stage

Control	Measure	Standard	Data Input	Interpretation
Firm Solvency	Number of financial ratios with strong indications divided by total number of ratios used	80%	Accounting and financial data	At least 80% of financial indicators must be strong for firm to be solvent
Firm Activities/ Organizational Definition Match	Number of activities incompatible with organizational definition	3	Various firmwide information	If three or more activities do not reflect firm definition, then time to redefine firm
Member Adjustment to Changes	Number of poor adjustments divided by total number of change adjustments per year	20%	Member questionnaire	If 20% or more of all adjustments to external or internal changes have negative effects, change mechanisms need be reexamined
Long-Term Survival	Positive indications on long-term factors divided by all long-term factors	80%	Member, consumer and advisor surveys	At least 80% of all long-term indicators must show positive responses
Firm Process/ Behavior Match	Successful tasks and behavior divided by total tasks and behavioral responses	60%	Member feedback and survey	In 60% or more instances, successful accomplishment followed successful behavior

Exhibit 9-30 Response to S.W.O.T.[1]

S.W.O.T.	Point of Discovery	Possible Response	Comments
Franchise Financing Shortage	Three months after franchise decision	• Seek sources of long-term financing • Redesign finance and accounting systems to handle franchise efforts • Control expenditures and reduce waste while not sacrificing member incentives • Encourage firmwide efforts to reduce shortage	
No Strategic Planning for Start-Ups	Two new places are not generating any demand	• Hold extended session with all members to deal with strategic planning shortcomings • Ensure start-up coordinators interface closely and with rest of firm • Redo lavational survey method to obtain more complete information • Select means to stimulate class enrollments	
Member Frictions	Five instances in as many months between old and new members	• Conduct survey of members individually concerning role of new and old members • Hold open forum to address problems discovered • Reach consensus on impacts and efforts members need to exert to adjust to the maturing of company • Pinpoint ways new members can assist older members and vice versa	

S.W.O.T.	Point of Discovery	Possible Response	Comments
Lack of Competition	Survey of existing "dance" franchises	• Expand quickly across the U.S. • Establish multiple franchise types • Penetrate certain local markets deeply • Formulate responses to handle entrance of dance competitors • Formulate strategic alternatives to effectively compete with nondance, leisure activities	
Surplus Demand	Market survey	• Discover activities which will draw many people as promotion event (dance concert, dance raffle, dance troupe tryouts, dance performance contest, etc.) • Expand outreach efforts through promotion and advertising • Establish summer dance trips, camp, tryouts, etc. • Sponsor regional dance performances and provide many participants	

[1]Competitive strengths and weaknesses and external opportunities and threats.

Chapter 10

Reaching Maturity and/or Reconception

SNAPSHOT

The firm has now reached an advanced stage of learning and development.

Starting with a good idea and a sound means of directing that idea into enterprising activities, the firm members have become aware of what problems, opportunities, strengths or weaknesses can and do arise in trying to fulfill the firm definition. They have seen the elements of operations all come together; the firm achieve initial success, attempt to expand, reach some critical decision points and emerge as a full-blown, weathered, growth-experienced organization. Now, supposedly the firm is mature. What this means is not any letting up of change occurrences, not an ability to just put the organization on auto-pilot and coast, and not a time to share the "spoils" of hard work and well-directed effort. Instead, this mature sense experienced by the firm members is a renewal of the entrepreneurial spirit which motivated the undertaking of the business at first. As well, there is a lot of knowledge and practice in seeking new challenges and innovations. So, past experience becomes a priceless guide to directly understanding and responding to the current situations faster and better than was done at the firm's outset. Further, if there is some "reward" for having reached this time in the firm's evolution it is legacy; that is, the ability to contribute inwardly and outwardly to the fulfillment of the firm and have that be at the same time an example for others to follow. This chapter will explore the means toward legacy and the implications of giving it.

STRATEGIC ISSUES FOR THE MATURITY
AND/OR RECONCEPTION STAGE

The orientation common to the issues presented below is organic; that is, the viewing of the organization as a self-correcting, integrative collective of members who seek to prevent problems and respond to changes.

The success of this organization is exactly correlated to the combined energies and accomplishments of all members. And, the major motivational force is to make more and varied contributions to society and all members simultaneously. In other terms, the original idea for the firm has now become an ideal within reach. Exhibit 10-1 sketches the primary strategic issues faced and coped with in this time frame.

A. Redefining the Firm. By the time an organization has reached this state of existence, many of its goals have been achieved, much of its mission satisfied, its objectives accomplished, reset and accomplished again in several cycles and thus, its purpose is fulfilled. In addition, the firm members have begun new activities and explored new interests which may not be reflected in the original definition. Thus, if not before, re-focusing of the firm "picture" is done. Exhibit 10-2 demonstrates what to consider in reconceptualizing the firm.

Exhibit 10-1 Strategic Issues to Reach Maturity and/or be Reconceived

- Does the firm need redefinition? If so, how will it be done?
- What new operating values, if any, are needed to propel the firm toward the long term?
- Are new avenues of carrying out social responsibility appropriate?
- If so, which ones?
- What, if any, competition might former firm members give?
- When and how might "intrapreneurship" be started?
- How would the firm do business with the public sector?
- Are there further needs to receive and give advice? What are they?
- How can problems be prevented?
- In what ways can leadership be enlarged?
- What new perspective can training have for the firm?
- Can work style and lifestyle be integrated? If so, how?
- In what ways can implementation activities be improved?
- What are the firm's competitive strengths and weaknesses?
- What are the firm's external opportunities and threats?
- Which controls can measure the firm's performance during this stage?

Sample Task 1

Now that you have redefined the firm, what means will you use to ensure that the new definition is "better" than the old? Will you continue to use these means into the foreseeable future? Why?

B. Creating New Operating Values. Exhibit 10-3 portrays a gamut of new sensibilities which can be brought to the firm to increase the exchange value of all transactions, interactions and growth experiences. Many of these insights might well have been with the firm since the beginning. Now, however, with other perceptions (discovered as the firm evolved) a synergistic impact occurs toward a stronger sense of values: overall, with the work group and by each individual.

Sample Task 2

What revisions of incentives and/or the work environment, if any, will you make to implement these new values? Why?

Exhibit 10-2 Reconceptualizing the Firm

I. Prelude
   A. Firm has started, achieved success, weathered crossroads activity and is now in mature stage
   B. Orientation is toward long-term survival
   C. Firm has reputation, culture and strategic planning framework
   D. Thrust is to modify and/or redefine definition to reflect current situation

II. Action
   A. Set time aside specifically to focus on firm definition
   B. Gather multiple inputs from members, shareholders, consumers, experts, financial and legal advisors and other interested parties
   C. Assess how closely firm "lives up to" actual definition
   D. Describe several visions of future survival
   E. Obtain consensus on which changes need to be made to definition
   F. Explore implications of changes on operations, strategic planning, culture, working environment, financial success, growth, and so forth
   G. Construct matrix of alternative definitions and impacts
   H. Choose composite revision to firm's purpose, goals, objectives and missions with steps needed to implement
   I. Use strategic planning to closely monitor subsequent changes

Exhibit 10-3 Creating New Operating Values

I. The Job
A. Learn to live with ambiguity
B. Be able to adjust to flexible responsibilities
C. Perceive work as a process not an end result
D. Balance creative and productive needs
E. Speak out constructively to improve your situation and the firm's concurrently

II. The Work Environment
A. View communication as both a means to transmit information and a way for personal growth
B. Consider decision making part of the larger process of resolving strategic issues
C. Exert efforts to have the organizational structure open new avenues of growth and achievement
D. Perceive that actions are based partially on "facts" and partially on "assumptions"
E. Understand that control is a means of creating more ways to be effective
F. Know that strategic planning is, at the same time, the plan and the process
G. Use information as a tool to create common vision and promote trust
H. Seek to prevent problems through early-warning means

III. The Work Group
A. Understand that no major concern can be dealt with effectively without the support and input of colleagues
B. Expect disagreements and turn them into sources of insight and stronger actions
C. Realize that autonomy means sharing with and trusting others
D. Come to grips with consensus and negotiation as stimuli for greater productivity
E. Know that successful actions are a combination of efficient decisions, shared responsibilities, and effective control
F. Define the corporate culture as a set of shared work assumptions used from idea to completed activity in an open, network pattern of communication
G. Build incentive programs around needs and desires of work group members

IV. The Consumer
A. Realize that a key source of improvement feedback can be gotten from your clients or customers
B. Strengthen ability to incorporate contingencies in communication and interaction with consumers
C. Be open to forming new relationships with buyers or suppliers; i.e., cooperative arrangement, barter, new business opportunities, etc.
D. Provide every channel possible for consumers to feel they are being individually served
E. Understand that what is provided to a consumer is a mix of product, quality and service

V. The Individual—You

A. Be cognizant of areas to explore toward self and professional improvement

B. Seek out ways to inspire and be inspired

C. Understand that accomplishments are as much about what is done as the manner in which it is done

D. Release tension and building trust through humor

E. Recognize the common purpose, your own goals and willing to balance the two

F. Look upon mistakes or difficult situations as opportunities toward stronger accomplishments

G. Balance work and personal lives to be mutually stimulating

H. Seek new or different thoughts, actions, ideas, or processes

I. Accepting of things as they are currently. Next, ask why, yet proceed to find out why not

J. Appreciate how mutually giving and receiving from others builds strong ties

K. Enjoy the everyday experiences with awe, pleasure and wonder

---

C. Upgrading Means of Social Responsibility. By this point in the firm's development, there is a clear track record of outreach activities. Thus, extending such achievements entails rethinking what is the mission and how it should function better for firm and society needs (see Exhibit 10-4). In a real sense, this process can result in a new "social contract" among firm members and a new "societal contract" between members of the firm and members of society. The "contracts" could be formal or informal, be detailed or general, and be conceptual or practical. Yet, common to any form, will be such elements as:

- background and rationale
- current actions
- guidance for future action
- areas for directing energies and resources

The "guidance for future action" section could be a set of principles delineating modes of behavior to emphasize and do. The principles would then serve as an ethical code "governing" behavior in many different situations. In addition, the code would stress modes of social action such as individual volunteering, formal corporate assistance, informal group projects, importance of time versus money and cooperative versus capitalistic ventures. The thrust is to become a firm of strong and varied contributions to social causes as one source of strengthening and sustaining a fine reputation.

Sample Task 3

What actions can you take to sustain an active use of social responsibility? How will these actions be different than what you have done before?

Exhibit 10-4 Upgrading Ways and Impacts of Social Responsibility

I. Current Status of Mission

    A. Past performance of socially responsible actions

    B. Strengths and weaknesses of mission

    C. Conflicts experienced in carrying out mission

II. Means of Revising Mission

    A. Improve fit between mission and other parts of firm definition

    B. Provide direct incentives for members to perform socially responsible actions

    C. Strengthen influence of firm culture on social responsibility

    D. Create new means to better identify and respond to socially responsible activities as direct benefits to firm

III. Organizational Options to Mission Revision

    A. Better integrated strategic planning function

    B. Productive public affairs/government relations group

    C. Member committee/suggestion means for stimulating greater involvement

    D. Outside expertise/guidance in improving role in society

    E. Advisory board of members and others to guide formulation and implementation of stronger mission

    F. Use professional association guidelines or examples of other companies

---

    D. Competition from Former Members. The time may arise when former firm members would set up "shop" to directly compete with your company. As Exhibit 10-5 aptly demonstrates, there are some precursor measures the firm and the former member can agree to in order to facilitate business without violation of trade secrets, patent rights, or other proprietary information. Although certain of these provisions are covered by state law, each case needs to be judged on its own merit. Thus, procedures should be enacted by the firm to prevent unwarranted abuses.

Sample Task 4

If the previous situation, competition from former members, arises, what role will you have and what role will your attorney have? Why?

    E. Instituting Intrapreneurship. A recent development among established companies, intrapreneurship is the formulation and execution of new ventures within an existing organization. Based on the fear of becoming "ever-less" competitive, maturing companies are seeking to provide incentives for members to innovate.

    Basically, this innovation takes two forms: with existing functions and with new activities. At times, new activities can grow out of changes

Exhibit 10-5 Acknowledging Competition from Former Members

I. Precautions

    A. Employment agreement specifying locations, time frame, business activities and resources may not be used to compete after member has left firm

    B. Discussion with member about to terminate concerning disclosing trade secrets, using confidential documents, entering into consumer contracts for personal gain, using proprietary customer or client lists or inducing other members to join new company

II. Activities member can do while preparing to leave

    A. Develop initial strategic plan

    B. Discuss new business with legal, financial and accounting advisors

    C. Order initial resources and rent space

    D. Informally describe business intentions with colleagues and current consumers

    E. Form business entity

III. Activities firm can do to encourage member interaction

    A. Provide promotion opportunities

    B. Establish "intrapreneurial" function to stimulate new business development in house

    C. Recognize that talented members may seek greener pastures and do not cause antagonism with them

    D. Seek to create amicable working relationship with new firm

to existing situations. However innovation comes about, generally a person or small group plan nurtures the idea to the point of producing better or new goods or services.

The intrapreneurs take the risk of not finding a market or developing a workable item and do put in some of their own money, but they still receive all the functional and resource support the firm can provide. However, this start-up mode allows the emerging venture to be tried on a limited basis first. If there are modifications to be made based on the feedback received, the innovation does not bankrupt the intrapreneurs while it is being refined. Further, to make the venture go, there needs to be two other factors operating:

- effective communication: interactive with feedback, cross-discipinary, interdepartmental and through several viewpoints.
- reliance on strategic planning: establish and maintain a project management system to interface when implementing the strategic activities.

A summary of the process with pros and cons is shown in Exhibit 10-6.

Exhibit 10-6 Instituting Intrapreneurship

I. Prerequisites

    A. Existing organization with achieved successes with original outputs, base of investment capital and interest in expanding into new ventures.

    B. Previous experience with buying companies and dissatisfaction with coordination

    C. High turnover of talented managers, engineers, artists, architects, accountants, marketeers, etc.

    D. Flexible organization structure and participative management

    E. Willing to provide sufficient incentives for intrapreneurs as well as firm assuming financial risks

    F. Willingness to consider ventures for: research and development of new items, marketing systems, financial consulting services, evaluation tools, technical, processes, etc.

II. Process

    A. Form venture committee to specify means for initiating new firm activities

    B. Solicit firm members to submit business proposals

    C. Evaluate and select those business ideas which have large potential for furthering firm definition

    D. Negotiate terms of capitalization and rewards with intrapreneurs

    E. Describe degree of control and monitoring which company will have with new venture

    F. Integrate successful venture into other company activities with further stimulation of new ventures

III. Advantages

    A. Efficient allocation of resources by proven and willing risk-takers

    B. Provides incentives for career advancement found in few other companies

    C. Performance rather than political acumen becomes basis for accomplishment

    D. Gives long-term opportunity to spawn, manage and spawn again new ventures—with proceeds for original ones

    E. Creates working environment of challenge and innovative direction within financially secure company

    F. Cornerstone for long-term viability of company

IV. Disadvantages

    A. Corporate structure unable to provide sufficient guidance and flexibility to ventures

    B. Items have insufficient demand due to lack of innovation marketing channels

    C. Inappropriate incentives for potential intrapreneurs

    D. Incomplete definition and evaluation of new venture prior to start-up

    E. Failure to consider intrapreneurship along with other growth options, or as next step once options are complete

Sample Task 5

Develop a pro-con chart for doing intrapreneurship. Do the cons outweigh the pros? Why?

F. Competing for Government Dollars. The public sector looms large, prevalent and lucrative on the horizon. Many entrepreneurs either do not know how or want to be involved with the government. However, given the federal, state or local presence in the business communities, going after contracts to provide your good or service can be another sustained revenue source at this stage of your life cycle. Exhibit 10-7 offers a thumbnail depiction of the process to become a contractor for the public sector. It is oriented toward the federal government, but works equally well for other types. The skills you require to obtain government work are three:
    • gaining entry to the right agencies and people
    • responding well to the solicitation
    • establishing a track record

    The first ability means deciding which way would the firm be best able to provide the items required under contract. The alternative "ways" of doing business with the federal government are
    • prime contractor, competitive procurement
    • prime contractor, noncompetitive procurement
    • set-aside or special programs
    • joint venture
    • subcontractor
    The second and third abilities mean what they imply: hard, honest, diligent and appropriate effort to satisfy the government client's requirements.

Sample Task 6

List the new set of skills you must have to compete for public sector dollars. Are you ready to learn them? Why?

G. Rethinking Advice. One of the seminal means to keep the influence database current is through receiving and giving advice. Why? Obtaining feedback and answers from knowledgeable and insightful people are two stimulants for enhancing the quality and use of the information needed to do strategic planning. Exhibit 10-8 portrays when and how to seek advice and give it also.
H. Preventing Problems. In many instances in our company "lives," problems are crises for immediate reaction. This book has shown how to

Exhibit 10-7 Doing Business with the Government Sector

I. **Orientation**
    A. Business done by contract
    B. Contracts awarded, in general, competitively
    C. Special considerations given to small and small, minority-owned businesses
    D. Procurement process takes time to award and up to 45 days for normal payment

II. **Preparation**
    A. Discover which products or services the government buys which you can provide
    B. Establish relationships with select government officials
    C. Enter firm on government solicitors list
    D. Learn what prerequisites, qualifications, requirements and standards you must meet before you can respond in general and specific to government procurement requests

III. **Response Decision**
    A. Receive and review solicitation
    B. Assess capabilities, interest and benefits of response
    C. If respond, prepare bid or proposal
    D. If do not respond, let officials know for further solicitations

IV. **Government Scrutiny**
    A. Be prepared for preaward survey, audit and/or negotiation of proposal
    B. If win, ensure that you have all necessary resources to perform work
    C. If lose, ask for debriefing

V. **Performance of Work**
    A. Obtain agreement on deliverables, due dates and payment schedule
    B. Perform work, submit reports as required and obtain feedback on progress
    C. Make any changes as deemed appropriate by the government or the government and you
    D. Submit final deliverables and make any necessary changes as necessary to have items accepted
    E. Send in voucher and receive final payment

VI. **Additional Topics**
    A. Noncompetitive procurement programs
    B. Subcontracting
    C. Further marketing

Exhibit 10-8 Rethinking Advice: Should It Be a Two-Way Street?

I. **When is advice to be sought?**
    A. Individual, department or firm does not have expertise to handle situation
    B. Expertise exists but is allocated to other projects
    C. An unbiased, objective perspective is sought
    D. Using the best help available could save more in the long run

II. **Attitude in seeking advice**
    A. Willing to acknowledge different viewpoint
    B. Understanding beforehand that changes may occur which advice seeker or other members may resist
    C. Realizing the need to establish rapport between advisor and members
    D. Conscientiously selecting well-qualified person to provide expertise
    E. Desiring a sustained effort at building effective communication with advisor
    F. Knowing that role is to learn while being the decision maker since further occurrence of the situation will be handled by you

III. **Giving advice**
    A. Can be done through speeches, lectures, demonstrations, roundtable discussions or other given to professional, trade or interest groups
    B. Can occur through "founders forum"—group of presidents who meet regularly to give and get insight about how to better direct and operate their company

solve problems before they become crises. Exhibit 10-9 describes how to prevent situations from becoming problems. A project management framework is a suggested tool to do so since it allows for systematic early detection and dissolution of negative impacts. But, as with solving problems, preventing them implies learning how to do so for future situations.

How many problems could not be prevented? If the second number is larger than the firsts, will Exhibit 10-9 prove of assistance? Why?

Sample Task 7

Inventory the problems you have solved in the past year. How many problems could not be prevented? If the second number is larger than the first, will Exhibit 10-9 prove of assistance? Why?

I. Enlarging Leadership Capacity. Exhibit 10-10 shows a diagnostic procedure for understanding current leadership practices in order to improve future leadership efforts. A key thrust is the development of a larger cadre of competent and well-qualified leaders for many and

Exhibit 10-9 Problem Prevention through Project Management

I. **Background**
    A. Initial sense of possible problem(s)
    B. Factors from influence database supporting A.
    C. Probable causes if problem(s) occur
    D. Previous attempts to deal with these problems or similar problems
    E. Benefits to be gained by exerting effort now versus costs of so doing

II. **Project Description**
    A. Reprise of problem(s) definition
    B. Resource requirements for prevention and solution
    C. Specific tools to map prevention activities (that is, alternative generation, scheduling, allocation, decision making and quality control techniques)
    D. Project team members, their duties, duration of activity, spokesperson, and coordination with other responsibilities
    E. Costs to achieve prevention and time frame to do so

III. **Project Fulfillment**
    A. Discover alternatives
    B. Articulate decision criteria and decision technique
    C. Choose viable alternatives
    D. Develop implementation, monitoring and control framework
    E. Apply framework to chosen alternatives, ensuring user support
    F. Verify results are preventing problem(s) and make any necessary modifications
    G. Use ouputs to strengthen other areas of firm

varying situations and the development of better leadership skills by all firm members applicable to specific situations as they arise.

Sample Task 8

How many members of your organization have leadership capabilities? How many members do not have it? How many members cannot learn or acquire it? Why?

J. Reeducating Training. The simple portrayal of Exhibit 10-11 has a direct message: not to allow training to lag behind the other progressive steps taken by the organization. That is, take another look at training to ascertain whether it is now an integral part of skill and consciousness-raising of each member or whether most of the growth insights still come from outside-the-firm experiences. If the latter pervades, then collectively expand the quality, types and levels of training offered. The philosophy is clear: training is not a luxury, for without it how can a firm advance?

Exhibit 10-10 Enlarging the Capacity for Leadership

I. **Background**

    A. Who are the leaders in the organization currently?

    B. Why are they leaders?

    C. What leadership influences has the organization felt from past leaders?

    D. Are these influences being used today? If so, how?

    E. What are the means through which new leaders can emerge?

II. **Diagnosis**

    A. Do the current leaders have the capacity to:

        1. Form an organizational vision and garner commitment for it

        2. Resolve past situations and view the present for what it is

        3. Guide members through recognizing and coping with change

        4. Gain cooperation and trust of others

        5. Motivate members to become part of something larger than themselves

        6. Create a working environment where individual genius and group efforts can co-exist

        7. Assist with resolving conflicts where appropriate, and

        8. Set an example for personal growth as well as learn from the examples of others

    B. What are the major strengths and weaknesses the "leaders" of this organization have or share?

    C. What efforts have been exerted to improve the strengths and resolve the weaknesses of leaders?

III. **Prognosis**

    A. Pinpoint areas where leadership and leadership training need to be improved

    B. Formulate alternative ways of accomplishing these improvements

    C. Select those alternatives which could best assist in achieving the firm's definition

    D. Implement alternatives as "pilot" projects and later on a firm wide basis

    E. Ensure that having better leaders is connected to organizational incentives and members' input

---

    K. Work Style/Lifestyle Integration. Most likely, this topic has been implicitly covered up until now. In case, however, there are any areas where work styles and lifestyles are out of balance, in conflict or not congruent, Exhibit 10-12 puts forth some suggested changes to the antiquated perspective in order to deal with these concerns.

Sample Task 9

What measures would you choose to assess work style/lifestyle integration? How would you apply them? Specify outcomes expected from using these measures. Do these differ from the actual work style/lifestyle integration which occurs? Why?

Exhibit 10-11 Giving "Training" a New Education

I. **Traditional View**
   A. Done only as needed to directly learn job skills
   B. Minimum investment by company
   C. Given infrequently

II. **Modified View**
   A. Train to level of job needs
   B. Use as incentive for higher productivity
   C. Becomes part of career development

III. **Enlightened View**
   A. Retraining is part and parcel of a person's career advancement
   B. Participant assists with design and orientation of training
   C. Outcomes provide opportunity for more innovation and job flexibility
   D. Training becomes activity which is major thread of firm success since any member is encouraged to give or receive training

Exhibit 10-12 Integrating Work Style with Lifestyle

I. **Background—traditional assumptions:**
   A. Work tasks are separate activities from personal habits or interests
   B. Work comes before pleasure
   C. Our identity, values and self-worth are primarily substantiated through the work organization
   D. Individuals are not to allow their personal lives to interfere with their professional lives

II. **Prognosis—new perspective:**
   A. Educate firm members in how their work lives can be enriched through integration with their personal lives
   B. Provide incentives and examples of recognizing early and dealing sensitively with negative effects of stress, diet, lifestyle, insufficient exercise, health, or other
   C. Encourage individual or group decisions about how to design and modify work environment
   D. Demonstrate and suggest changes to daily work rhythm to attain higher productivity while still retaining high energy level

L. Implementation Improvements. Clearly, the second most important facet to strategic planning after identifying issues is doing something constructive about them. Since implementation of alternatives to take proper care of strategic issues is a well-worn function by this stage, why would Exhibit 10-13 need to be written?

The answer is that even with the positive impacts the firm has felt, there are quite possibly still weak facets to implementation. In addition, mistakes may be occurring in selecting the type of implementation appropriate, for example, actions or practices or projects and the level of coordination (individual, group, intergroup or a mixture). Third, shortcomings can also be found in how controls are used, the results evaluated and responses taken to such results. Finally, how modifications arise and are dealt with and what input eventually is used to redo strategic plans are two relatively unpracticed areas for further training. The bottom line to continuity for strategic planning is having well-understood experience and practice as a prelude to coping with the next set of issues that arises.

Sample Task 10

Come up with a procedure to feed implementation results directly into the next strategic planning cycle. What impacts will this procedure have for increasing the usefulness of doing strategic planning?

Exhibit 10-13 Improving Implementation Activities

I. Types of Activities
  A. Acts—fundamental and immediate behavior
  B. Actions—sequences of acts
  C. Practice—series or parallel sets of actions
  D. Project—system or practices

II. Results from Activities
  A. Expected; unexpected
  B. High performance; low performance
  C. Easily corrected; difficult to modify
  D. Short-term effects; longer-term impacts
  E. Relates well to other activities; relates poorly to other activities

III. Areas to Increase Implementation Effectiveness
  A. Decision criteria and/or technique
  B. Scheduling and coordination
  C. Controlling and evaluation
  D. Modification
  E. Input to reformulation of strategic plans

M. Competitive Strengths and Weaknesses. External Opportunities and Threats.

As before in prior chapters, these are covered below with the "live" firm example.

N. Performance Controls. Exhibit 10-14 illustrates what some of the overall measures of firm viability are. Each is used to assess how well all members collectively are effectively doing strategic planning during this stage.

O. The summary of strategic planning and the document produced for the firm during this mature or reconceptual stage is given in Exhibit 10-15.

STRATEGIC PLAN IN ACTION

At this juncture, Coplan's School of Dance is undergoing a fundamental rethinking of its purpose, mission, goals and objectives and direction. As Exhibit 10-17 shows, the organization is stressing a balance between behavior and process, accomplishment and change, and growth and stability.

The major new direction being explored is how new ventures can be spawned by the fertile work environment. These ventures provide additional entrepreneurial challenge and excitement to enhancing the viability of the organization for the foreseeable future. In addition, new relationships are established with competing former members. Along with new activities come new values which add to the stroking and creativity which pervade the everyday workplace. Further, on the process "scale," increased emphasis is placed on preventing rather than solving problems and upgrading implementation activities. On the other "scale," behavior is enhanced through enlarging leadership opportunities and skills, providing a new training perspective for all members, and closely but sensitively monitoring the integration of member work styles with lifestyles. These issues are are addressed in Exhibit 10-16. The time frame is eighteen months since in this time period the new directions will be completed (see Exhibit 10-18).

Exhibit 10-14 Measuring Control during This Stage

- Degree of response to change
- Diversity of member satisfactions
- Degree of problem prevention
- Level of long-term viability
- Ability to institute improvements
- Strength of firm redefinition
- Degree of innovation
- Improvement in leadership
- Work style/lifestyle integration

Exhibit 10-15 Strategic Plan for the Maturity and/or Reconception Stage: Elements

I.　**Firm Definition**

II.　**Influence Database**

III.　**Strategic Issues and Alternatives**
   A.　Firm redefinition
   B.　New operating values
   C.　Social responsibility expansion
   D.　Former firm member competition
   E.　Establishing intrapreneurship
   F.　Public sector clients
   G.　Advice extensions
   H.　Problem prevention
   I.　Leadership enlargement
   J.　New training perspective
   K.　Work style/lifestyle integration
   L.　Implementation improvement
   M.　Competitive strengths and weaknesses
   N.　External opportunities and threats
   O.　Overall performance controls

IV.　**Decision Criteria**

V.　**Selection of Alternatives**

VI.　**Implementation of Alternatives**
   A.　Time table
   B.　Summary of positive and negative attributes

VII.　**Monitoring**
   A.　Feedback
   B.　Control methods

The controls used here are "macro"—they apply to measuring the entire organization's performance. Some possibilities of controls are given in Exhibit 10-19. Finally, ways of dealing with the strengths, opportunities, weaknesses and threats Coplan's School of Dance is likely to face are presented in Exhibit 10-20. As with the previous stages, existing strategic issues, control indications and competitive strengths and weaknesses or external opportunities and threats will form the nucleus of the subsequent strategic planning effort. Are you prepared to make it happen?

Exhibit 10-16 Strategic Issues and Alternatives for the Maturity/Reconception Stage of Coplan's School of Dance

Issue	Strategic Alternative(s)	Reasons	Comments
Firm Redefinition	• Minor modifications • Major modifications • Total redesign	• For long-term survival • To have stronger correlation between actions and desires • In order to create climate for greater member actualization • For increased success in responding to change	See Exhibit 10-17
New Operating Values	• Having more autonomy based on greater learning accomplishments • Using controls as means to improve not disprove • Continual emphasis on seeking better information and using it better • Having feedback become integral to most practices and all projects • Ensuring all members want and know how to strategically plan, negotiate, lead, and arrive at consensus • Have corporate culture be "open" rather than "closed" system • Listen as much as speak with your consumers • Strive to improve already high quality of outputs • Accept and make the most of contingencies	• Continued growth of members • Broadening competitive position • Stronger abilities to harness and apply resources • Provide self-integrating capability for firm	

Issue	Strategic Alternative(s)	Reasons	Comments
	• Coming to understand that the long-term incentives are more qualitative (satisfaction and inspiration) than quantitative (money and status) • Finding ways to use humor • Allowing work and personal lives to mutually reinforce each other		
Social Responsibility	• Establish special dance program for abused children	• To begin to fulfill revised mission • To expand current reputation	
Expansion	• Donate no less than 8% of post-tax profits to community activities • Every firm member in all franchises does at least one day per month of social action	• Provide another avenue for member involvement	
Former Member Competition	• Ignore activities • Ensure no provisions of termination agreement are violated • Try to work on projects of mutual interest	• Short time frame • Large negative impacts possible if have no response • Potential improvements to firm functions	

(*continued*)

Exhibit 10-16 (Continued)

Issue	Strategic Alternative(s)	Reasons	Comments
Establishing Intrapreneurship	• Provide institute for new dance "games"	• Channel for certain firm members' energies • Potential new source of revenue • Keep creative people as firm members • Can implement on limited basis first • Cost and time are small to begin activity	
Public Sector			Not at this time
Advice Extensions	• Ensure that members individually or in groups are giving and receiving advice at least twice a month in each area	• Source of feedback • Strengthen communication skills • Tap into latest thinking or technique • Improve firm operations • Time and cost are minimal	
Problem Prevention	• Franchise coordination • Cost reduction on benefits package	• Source of chronic illness • Affect financial and motivational solvency • Prior failures with not "catching the problem in the bud"	

Issue	Strategic Alternative(s)	Reasons	Comments
Leadership Enlargement	• Provide leadership classroom and on-the-job training • Have leadership activities—expected and unexpected—become part of the performance review	• Outgrowth of operating values • Means of member growth • Connection to other responsibilities, sense of self and satisfaction • Strengthen "internal" firm reputation	
New Training Perspective	• All members have at least three training experiences each year	• Improve member abilities • Sustain current perspective • Source of new firm activities, information, members and techniques	
Work Style/ Lifestyle Integration	• Set minimum-maximum limits for work activities with counterbalancing suggestions from lifestyle	• Have healthier, higher motivated members • Early warning system to discover member concerns and deal with them before crisis point is reached • Reduce costs incurred by unhealthy lifestyle practices	

(continued)

Exhibit 10-16 (Continued)

Issue	Strategic Alternative(s)	Reasons	Comments
Implementation Improvement	• Ensure periodic reassessment of monitoring function	• Reduce ineffective execution of strategic alternatives • Upgrade early warning device for member dissatisfaction, inability, cost escalation, etc. • Strengthen strategic planning process • Useful for any implementation situation	
Competitive Strengths and Weaknesses	+ Franchising is successful + Turnover is almost zero + Incentives are being enlarged all the time + Firm seeking new directions + Reputation is growing - Cost accounting system is ineffective - Interoffice communication technology is antiquated - Scheduling capacity for classes is at the limit - Paperwork is lowering instruction productivity - Firmwide get-togethers are sparse	• Correct shortcomings to sustain strengths • Thrust is for long-term existence • Use early warning system to dissolve ills	

Issue	Strategic Alternative(s)	Reasons	Comments

External Opportunities and Threats	• Major dance franchise is considering liquidation
	• Two former members are organizing dance "Olympics"
	• Enough money in stock and profit-sharing plans to purchase "retreat" estate (which needs to be sold quickly)
	• Dance wear manufacturer needs capital. Willing to have firm become partner
	• Approached by local public TV station to do special on firm and its community outreach
	  - Former member franchising dance wear stores
	  - Major competitor has begun late-night TV ads
	  - Attorney died suddenly
	  - Franchise vandalized
	  - Bank where firm has business accounts is undergoing reorganization
		• Use scanning system to detect and respond early to new marketplace developments
		• Have contingency plans ready to use
		• Affect firm's increasing ability to handle change	

Controls	• Emphasis on overall performance measures
	• Use specific, functional measures to validate overall measures' results
		• Improve capability to:
		  - change performance
		  - change standard
		  - do both
		  - do neither or
		  - do something else	

Exhibit 10-17 Redefinition of Coplan's School of Dance

I. Purpose. To provide an array of dance movement and exercise classes to a variety of consumer groups on a franchise basis.

II. Goals
  A. To create an integrative learning environment where different ages and different experience levels can share and further their abilities
  B. To have a successful mix of standard and custom-tailored learning activities
  C. Each instructor can improve his or her abilities and satisfactions on an ongoing basis
  D. To evolve an organization completely managed, directed and stimulated by the mutual input and feedback of all members
  E. To continue to innovate ideas for instruction, dance wear, exercise, new dance activities and better business operations
  F. To have the strategic planning done herein become an example for other firms to successfully use
  G. To effectively and consistently integrate short-term actions into long-term effects

III. Objectives
  A. To maintain a profit level of 10% or more over the next eighteen months
  B. To successfully institute major improvements to identified weaknesses in the work environment over the next year
  C. To open four privately owned franchises in the next nine months
  D. To ensure firm investments yield, on average, no less than 10% for the next year and a half
  E. To open the doors to the Institute for New Dance Games at the end of the third quarter of this year
  F. To complete the firm redefinition in no more than three months
  G. To prevent three major problems from occurring in the next six months

IV. Mission
  A. To encourage each firm member to spend at least 10% of each month's "free time" in community service
  B. To expand time and resources devoted to community activities
  C. To advocate certain positions on health, interest groups, business ethics to legislative bodies, associations and civic and professional groups
  D. To be continually responsive to the collective desires of firm members
  E. To increase barter activities
  F. To develop early warning capability for identifying and assessing social concerns in order to suggest responses and give level of firm involvement with those responses
  G. To provide means of having community projects specified and carried out by teams of instructors, students and adults

Exhibit 10-18 Time Table to Reach Long-Term Survival

Activity	Time frame										
	Month 1	Month 2	Month 3	Month 4	Month 5	Month 6	Month 7	Month 8	Month 9	...	Month 18
Redefine firm	——										
Create new operating values	————										
Expand social responsibility	————————————										
Establish intrapreneurship	————————————————————										
Prevent problems	————————————————————————————										
Enlarge leadership	————————————————————————————————										
More training	——										
Improve implementation	——										
Coordinate franchises	——										

Exhibit 10-19 Using Controls during the Maturity/Reconception Stage

Control	Measure	Standard	Data Input	Interpretation
Response to Change	Number of change responses divided by total number of changes	60%	Influence database	Shows how many of the important changes affecting the firm were responded to
Problem Prevention	Number of prevented problems divided by total number of problems	3:1	Member survey	For every problem, three problems should be prevented
Long-Term Viability	Number of long-term practices or projects divided by total number of practices or projects	50%	Implementation records	For every two projects, at least one will have long-term impacts
Institute Improvements	Number of improvements divided by number of areas requiring them	70%	Observations and operations records	At least 70% of all required areas have improvements carried out
Firm Redefinition	Number of positive consequences divided by number of negative consequences	2:1	Member questionnaire	For every negative outcome at least two positive outcomes occur
Innovation	Number of innovations per strategic planning period	10	Influence database	At least 10 innovations occur from one to the next cycle of strategic planning
Leadership Improvement	Number of improvements divided by number of leadership activities	15%	Influence database	At least 15% of all leadership is geared toward improvement
Work Style/ Lifestyle Integration	Range for balance for work/life factors	Varies for each work factor	Work style committee	Interpret to ascertain whether member lives are out of balance

Exhibit 10-20 Response to S.W.O.T.[1]

S.W.O.T.	Point of Discovery	Possible Response	Comments
Ineffective cost accounting system	IRS decision to audit	• Call in consultant to redesign better system • Ask accountant to correct problem • Purchase compatible computer software to handle situation • Do nothing	
Antiquated communication technology	Backlog of concerns needing quick response	• Call in consultant to redesign system • Institute office automation—standard program • Institute office automation—custom tailored program • Use existing system more fully	
Maximum class scheduling capacity	Have three operating hours per week where class areas not used	• Raise rates slightly to reduce demand slightly • Rent space in other quarters • Expand working hours	
Lowered instruction productivity	Instructors spend 40% of time on paperwork	• Reduce paperwork requirements • Obtain more clerical support to handle instructor paperwork • Have many requirements automated for ease of information entry	
Firmwide socializing has decreased	Three events in last year	• Schedule more events • Emphasize more office-based events • Encourage folks with common interests across all offices to advertise these and meet	

(continued)

Exhibit 10-20 (Continued)

S.W.O.T.	Point of Discovery	Possible Response	Comments
Competitor liquidation	Local newspaper article	• Ignore • Wait until bankruptcy occurs and then purchase assets • Acquire franchise new	
Dance Olympics	Informal discussions	• Offer to be sponsor and contribute to dance "team" • Use involvement as promotion of social responsibility	
Purchase "retreat" estate	Member suggestion	• No action • Find and purchase now • Find and purchase later • Find, lease and then purchase • Explore several possible sites and decide which one is best	
Investment in dance wear manufacturer	Promotional mailing	• No action • Give loan • Become equity partner • Obtain equity and generate loan • Establish priority marketing effort with Co-plan's being primary retailer	

S.W.O.T.	Point of Discovery	Possible Response	Comments
Franchise competition	Promotion mailing	• Closely monitor activities and prepare contingency responses • Upgrade quality of marketing and merchandise for dance wear	
Competitor T.V. ads	T.V. viewing a partner	• Do nothing since majority of consumers would not likely see them	
Attorney death	Phone call from a partner	• Continue with other partners of law firm • Find new counsel • Continue with present law firm until decide on next attorney	
Franchise vandalized	Self-inspection	• Ensure insurance will cover damage • Assess damages and use contingency plan to resolve them • Conduct firmwide meeting on security and safety	
Bank reorganization	Phone call from V.P. of bank	• Do nothing • Move account(s) to new investment institution • Consider means of optional return on account monies through distribution with several establishments	

[1]Competitive strengths and weaknesses and external opportunities and threats.

Index

About the Author

Steven Stryker, president of Stryker Associates, has thirty-three years of experience in providing technical assistance, facilitation, and training in strategic planning, project management and acquisition, and contracting arenas. He has been in the forefront of combining the above three areas of expertise to ensure that timely, complete, and effective performance occurs in information technology, technical support and logistics, research and development, commercial services or a combination. Working with both private- and public-sector clients, the results from these efforts (singularly or in combination) have saved time, money, and problems, while obtaining higher-quality results.

Besides the republishing of *Plan to Succeed: A Guide to Strategic Planning*, Roman & Littlefield is also republishing *Guide to Successful Consulting* and *Principles and Practices of Professional Consulting*. He has also published *The COTR Handbook: Effective Catalyst for Stronger Organizational* Performance, which demonstrates effective contract processes and practices. Recently he contributed a chapter on research and development contracting for a forthcoming book on services contracting.

In addition, over the past three years, Mr. Stryker has been a requested speaker and presenter at a number of conferences and seminars on performance-based topics (with a focus on enhancing performance application and accountability).

CPSIA information can be obtained at www.ICGtesting.com
Printed in the USA
BVOW071245260212

283695BV00004B/3/P